DNA IDENTIFICATION AND EVIDENCE:
APPLICATIONS AND ISSUES

DNA IDENTIFICATION AND EVIDENCE: APPLICATIONS AND ISSUES

ERIC A. FISCHER AND NANCY LEE JONES

Novinka Books
Huntington, New York

Senior Editors: Susan Boriotti and Donna Dennis
Coordinating Editor: Tatiana Shohov
Office Manager: Annette Hellinger
Graphics: Wanda Serrano
Book Production: Matthew Kozlowski, Jonathan Rose and Jennifer Vogt
Circulation: Cathy DeGregory, Ave Maria Gonzalez and Raheem Miller
Communications and Acquisitions: Serge P. Shohov

Library of Congress Cataloging-in-Publication Data
Available Upon Request

ISBN 1-56072-972-4.

Copyright © 2001 by Novinka Books
A Division of Nova Science Publishers, Inc.
227 Main Street, Suite 100
Huntington, New York 11743
Tele. 631-424-6682   Fax 631-424-4666
E Mail Novascil@aol.com

All rights reserved. No part of this book may be reproduced, stored in a retrieval system or transmitted in any form or by any means: electronic, electrostatic, magnetic, tape, mechanical photocopying, recording or otherwise without permission from the publishers.

The authors and publisher have taken care in preparation of this book, but make no expressed or implied warranty of any kind and assume no responsibility for any errors or omissions. No liability is assumed for incidental or consequential damages in connection with or arising out of information contained in this book.

This publication is designed to provide accurate and authoritative information with regard to the subject matter covered herein. It is sold with the clear understanding that the publisher is not engaged in rendering legal or any other professional services. If legal or any other expert assistance is required, the services of a competent person should be sought. FROM A DECLARATION OF PARTICIPANTS JOINTLY ADOPTED BY A COMMITTEE OF THE AMERICAN BAR ASSOCIATION AND A COMMITTEE OF PUBLISHERS.

Printed in the United States of America

Contents

Preface vi

DNA Identification: Applications and Issues 1
    Abstract 1
    Summary 1
    Introduction 3
    Why DNA Can Be Used in Identification 4
    How DNA Is Used in Identification 6
    Databases 13
    Federal Agency Programs and Activities 14
    Relevant Public Laws 21
    Current and Emerging Issues 22
    Relationship of DNA Identification of Medical Genetic Testing 30

DNA Evidence: Legislative Initiatives in the 106th Congress 37
    Summary 37
    Introduction 38
    Features of DNA Evidence 39
    Prior Federal Law 40
    Legislative Issues 42
    Other Issues 61
    Legislation 63

Index 73

PREFACE

This book provides an overview of how the genetic information contained in DNA is used for identification, and a discussion of issues associated with those uses. It begins by discussing the unique properties of genetic information that make it a powerful tool for identification and what is involved in making identifications from DNA. Next is a description of current federal programs and activities, followed by discussion of issues raised by the development of this new technology. Major issues include the use of DNA identification in the criminal justice system (including sample backlogs, databases, and postconviction DNA analysis), impacts of technological improvements, and privacy.

DNA evidence is a powerful forensic tool in criminal cases. Its use and capabilities have increased substantially since it was first introduced in the late 1980s. A DNA profile may provide powerful evidence in many criminal investigations, either to incriminate or exculpate a suspect. DNA evidence is very stable and can be extracted and profiled from a sample many years after being deposited. The technologies used are increasingly sensitive, powerful, fast, and cost-effective. The cost of performing analyses and the time required continue to decline. Those features of the technology are likely to continue to improve over the next decade.

DNA IDENTIFICATION: APPLICATIONS AND ISSUES

Eric A. Fischer

ABSTRACT

This report provides an overview of how the genetic information contained in DNA is used for identification, and a discussion of issues associated with those uses. It begins by discussing the unique properties of genetic information that make it a powerful tool for identification and what is involved in making identifications from DNA. Next is a description of current federal programs and activities, followed by discussion of issues raised by the development of this new technology. Major issues include the use of DNA identification in the criminal justice system (including sample backlogs, databases, and postconviction DNA analysis), impacts of technological improvements, and privacy.

SUMMARY

DNA technology can provide useful identifying information in many situations, such as in solving crimes, determining paternity, and identifying human remains. Research is resulting in improvements in sensitivity and power and reductions in cost. Such use and improvements are raising several policy issues.

The use of DNA in identification results from its unique characteristics. It is a complex molecule, containing much information. Each person has billions of identical copies. The structure of the molecule varies from person to person and is inherited, so the DNA of relatives is more similar than that of unrelated people. Also, DNA is easily preserved with the structure intact.

Identification requires comparing DNA whose source has not been determined with DNA whose source is known. The first step is to characterize corresponding DNA sequences from samples. The resulting profiles are then compared. If they differ, the samples did not have the same origin. If they match, then they could have come from the known source, or from someone else who has an identical profile. The science of population genetics provides ways of estimating quantitatively the chances that the matched DNA could have come from another source.

Databases or indexes are often used in DNA identification. They might contain profiles of persons whose identity is known, such as convicted felons, or whose identity is not known, such as from crime scene samples or unidentified remains. The Combined DNA Index System (CODIS), administered by the FBI, contains both kinds. When a profile is obtained from a relevant sample, the database can be searched to determine if a match is found. Thus, a suspect may be identified when a profile from a crime-scene is searched against profiles of convicted felons.

Congress has enacted several laws relating to DNA evidence. The DNA Identification Act of 1994 (P.L. 103-322) authorized CODIS and a grants program for state and local laboratories, and addressed quality control and privacy issues. The Antiterrorism and Effective Death Penalty Act of 1996 (P.L. 104-132) expanded CODIS and established a grants program that required states, to be eligible, to collect DNA samples from persons convicted of felony sex crimes. The Crime Identification Technology Act of 1998 (P.L. 105-521) established a grants program that funds a broad range of activities, including several related to DNA typing. The national Institute of Justice (NIJ) and the Bureau of Justice Assistance (BJA) administer those and other relevant grants programs. The National Institute of Standards and Technology (NIST), the Armed Forces Institute of Pathology (AFIP), and the Army Criminal Investigation laboratory (USACIL) also have significant DNA identification activities.

Policy issues raised by the use of DNA in identification include how best to eliminate the large backlog of samples awaiting processing for CODIS, whether to broaden the offenses that quality, how to respond to the increasing number of requests for postconviction DNA analysis, how to address privacy issues, and what impacts the broadening applications of the technology may have.

INTRODUCTION

As our understanding of human genetics has become more and more sophisticated, scientists have developed increasingly powerful tools using genetic information to aid in identifying individual people. DNA can be helpful in many situations where identification is at question: For example, in criminal cases, forensic DNA evidence can link a suspect, or a weapon such as a knife, to a crime scene. It can also exclude a suspect. The best known sources of DNA evidence are blood and semen, but increasingly it can be obtained from other items, such as a bottle cap, a toothbrush, a bite mark on a piece of cake, or a fragment of a contact lens. Another use is to identify human remains, such as of a soldier killed in battle. Or it might be used to determine biological relationship, such as in paternity cases. This report focuses on using human DNA to determine individual identify, but animal and plant can also be used, to identify species (for example, did a sample of meat come from a protected whale species?) or even individuals (did a seed pod found in a truck come from a particular tree at a crime scene?).[1]

Those and similar developments raise several policy issues, including the use of genetic information in the criminal justice system, the impacts of continuing technological improvements, and the effects of the technology on privacy and individual rights. This report provides an overview of how genetic information is used in identification and some of the issues associated with those uses. It begins by discussing the unique properties of genetic information that make it a powerful tool for identification and what is involved in making identifications from physical evidence. Next is a description of current federal programs and activities related to DNA

---

[1] The examples in parentheses refer to real cases. The first involved testing whale meat purchased in markets in Japan – C.S. Baker & S.R. Palumbi, "Which Whales Are Hunted? A Molecular Genetic Approach to Monitoring Whaling," *Science 265* (1994): 1538. The second was a 1993 murder case in which the DNA in seed pods in a defendant's truck were found to match the DNA of a palo verde tree at the crime scene – G. Sensabaugh and D.H. Kaye, "Non-human DNA Evidence," *Jurimetrics Journal 38* (1998): 1-16.

identification, followed by discussion of issues raised by the development of this new technology.

WHY DNA CAN BE USED IN IDENTIFICATION

The use of DNA in identification – sometimes called DNA typing or DNA profiling[2] – results from its unique characteristics. Those characteristics also affect how it can be used and the issues that arise from using it. Key features are described below.

It is a complex molecule, containing much information. DNA is a chemical, deoxyribonucleic acid, consisting of modular components, called nucleotides, that are connected in a linear sequence. Each nucleotide contains one of four bases – called adenine, dytosine, guanine, and thymine, often designated by their initials A, C, G, and T. Each DNA molecule consists of two complementary strands with each adenine on one strand paired with a thymine on the other, and each guanine with a cytosine. The sequence of bases strung along a DNA molecule contains the information that forms the basis of the genetic code of humans and most other organisms.[3] Much of the growing body of knowledge about DNA comes from efforts of the Human Genome Project, a major goal of which is to create a map of the code and identify the sequence of bases on the DNA molecule.[4] DNA identification technologies tap a small part of the large set of information that the molecule contains.

---

[2] It is sometimes also called DNA testing. In this report, for clarity, that term is used only to refer to medical tests.

[3] For a more in-depth description, see Human Genome Program, U.S. Department of Energy, *Primer on Molecular Genetics* (Washington, DC, 1992), [http://www.ornl.gov/hgmis/publicat/primer/primer.pdf].

[4] The Human Genome Project is an international effort performed with both government and private funding. The U.S. federal effort began in 1988 with the signing of a memorandum of understanding between the Department of Energy (DOE) and the National Institutes of Health (NIH). At DOE, the program is housed in the office of Biological and Environmental Research (OBER) within the Office of Science (see the DOE genome project website at [http:/www.sc.doe.gov/production/ober/hub_top.html] for more information). At NIH, the program resides in the National Human Genome Research Institute, NHGRI (see the NHGRI website [http://222.nhgri.nih.gov:90/ index.html] for more information). NHGRI was established by statute, under the name National Center for Human Genome Research, in the National Institutes of Health Revitalization Act of 1993 (P.L. 103-43). The DOE genome efforts do not have separate statutory authorization.

Each person has billions of identical copies of DNA in the cells of the body. Most of the billions of cells in a person's body contain identical sets of DNA molecules[5] – approximately 3 billion base-pairs per cell altogether. Most of the DNA is contained in 23 pairs of chromosomes in the nuclei of cells. Within each pair, one chromosome is inherited from the mother and the other from the father. Some DNA, inherited only from the mother, is also contained outside the cell nucleus, in structures called mitochondria, which are small bodies with many copies in each cell. Because the human body contains so many copies of DNA, even a very small amount of body fluids or tissues, such as blood or skin, can yield useful identifying information.

The structure of the molecule, and therefore the information it contains, varies from person to person. DNA sequences from any two people will be the same at many points along the DNA molecule, but the overall nuclear DNA sequence of each person is unique, except for identical twins, who have identical DNA.[6] On a single chromosome, individual *alleles*, which are discrete components of a DNA sequence, are inherited intact. Each pair of chromosomes has many pairs of alleles[7] (the total number is as yet unknown), with one member of the pair inherited from the father and the other from the mother. The region of a pair of chromosomes containing a pair of alleles is called a *locus*. The DNA of the two alleles inherited at any particular locus may have identical or different base-pair sequences.[8] It is the substantial variation in DNA among people that is characterized with the technologies used in DNA identification.

The structure is inherited, so the DNA of close relatives is more similar than that of distant relatives or unrelated people. Since half of a person's

---

[5] The major exceptions are germ cells (eggs, sperm, and their precursors) which have 23 single, not paired, chromosomes, and red blood cells, which have no DNA. DNA extracted from blood comes from white blood cells. The DNA sequences in different germ cells are not identical, because each contains half the full DNA complement, partially mixed through a process called recombination. Also, rare changes, called mutations, can occur in a sequence through damage, errors in replication, or other means. Only mutations that occur in the germ call line can be inherited – they are called germ-line mutations; all others are called somatic mutations.

[6] except for mutations and certain other minor variations.

[7] except for the sex chromosomes in males (see below).

[8] The technical term is *homozygous* if they are identical and *heterozygous* if they are different.

DNA comes from each parent,[9] full siblings also share half their alleles, on average, and grandparents and first cousins, one quarter. However, since a son receives his Y chromosome from his father, all the alleles on that chromosome are identical to the father's and are inherited through the paternal line alone.[10] Similarly, all alleles in mitochondria are identical to the mother's and are inherited through the maternal line alone.[11] Therefore, the mitochondrial DNA of a male, for example, will be identical to that of his maternal grandmother, and his Y-chromosome DNA identical to that of his paternal grandfather. The inheritance patterns of DNA mean that analyzing a person's DNA can also provide identifying information about a relative.

Most of a person's DNA has no known biological function. Genes are segments of DNA that contain the code for making specific chemicals (mostly proteins). Humans have tens of thousands of genes (the exact number is not yet known), but they comprise only a small part of a person's DNA, most of which has no known function. However, many nonfunctional segments of a person's DNA can be characterized with the techniques of molecular biology; those segments are called *markers*. The distinction between genes and markers has implications for use in identification that will be discussed later.

DNA is easily preserved with the structure intact. DNA is a surprisingly stable chemical, and sequences can be easily preserved intact in dried or frozen samples. However, DNA can be degraded, particularly in warm or moist environments or in the presence of many common chemicals. The ability to use DNA in identification depends both on the size and the condition of the sample. That has consequences for sample collection, handling, and storage in applications such s law enforcement.

HOW DNA IS USED IN IDENTIFICATION

Using DNA in identification requires comparing DNA whose source has not been determined (such as from a crime scene or from a child in a

---

[9] Exceptions are mitochondrial DNA and the sex chromosomes in males, in whom the Y chromosome is much smaller than the X and contains many fewer alleles.

[10] The power of using this male-line inheritance of the Y-chromosome was demonstrated in the genetic research that provided strong support for the assertion that Thomas Jefferson fathered at least one son by Sally Hemings – Eugene A. Foster and others, "Jefferson Fathered Slave's Last Child," *Nature* 396 (1998) 27-28.

[11] except for mutations.

paternity case) with DNA whose source is known (such as from a suspect or from a putative father). Four basic steps are involved: characterization, comparison, calculation, and interpretation. They are each discussed below, along with implications for applications and issues.

Characterization

The first step is to characterize or profile corresponding DNA sequences in the samples to be compared. For forensic evidence in a criminal case, one or more samples of blood, semen, or other sources of DNA related to the crime will be processed, as will usually a sample from one or more suspects. It is not possible with current technology to characterize the entire DNA sequence. Instead, alleles at specific loci are characterized. The technique used depends on the particular kind of marker. The major kinds of markers in use today are VNTRs, STRs, mtDNA, and certain simpler sequences.

For most of the fifteen years during which DNA typing has been used in forensics, VNTRs (variable number of tandem repeats) have been the major kind of marker used. They have the greatest potential power to identify or exclude, because they vary more from person to person than any other DNA system used in identification. They consist of sections of DNA in which a sequence of about 15-70 bases is repeated many times. Analysis of a sample using VNTRs measures the approximate number of repetitions in each marker examined. That number varies substantially from person to person. Analysis of VNTRs uses RFLP[12] technology, which requires that substantially more DNA be present, and in good condition, in the sample than do the other systems described below. Therefore, many samples that are degraded or have very small amounts of DNA cannot be processed using VNTRs.

STRs (short tandem repeats) also consist of repeated sequences, but the number of bases repeated is smaller (2-4), as is the total length of DNA comprising an allele (approximately 100-300 bases for STRs versus 500-10,000 VNTRs). STRs are not as variable as VNTRs, and therefore more

---

[12] RFLP stands for *restriction fragment length polymorphism*. A chemical called a restriction enzyme cuts the DNA molecule in certain (restricted) places corresponding to particular base sequences. The result is pieces of DNA called *restriction fragments* that vary among people – are *polymorphic* – in *length*. RFLP and VNTR are sometimes used interchangeably to refer to the analysis of VNTRs using RFLP technology.

loci must be types to obtain the same resolving power as with VNTRs.[13] Nevertheless, STRs can be examined with much smaller samples (for example, requiring a bloodstain the size of a pinhead rather than one the size of a quarter coin), for two reasons. First, DNA-amplification procedures (known as PCR – the polymerase chain reaction) can be used. The process uses the ability of DNA to replicate itself to make many identical copies from a small initial amount of DNA. The procedure does not yet work with VNTRs. Second, because the sequences are shorter, they are less likely to be damaged if the sample is degraded. Therefore, such samples can often yield more usable results with STRs than with VNTRs. STRs also have some other technical advantages over VNTRs. In particular, they can be processed in the laboratory much more quickly and they are easier to interpret. For those reasons, STRs, which first became available for forensic use a few years ago, are quickly replacing VNTRs as the standard marker for typing.

Mitochondrial DNA (mtDNA) can be used in even smaller or more degraded samples than STRs. That is because the relevant DNA sequences are moderately short (approximately 1,200 bases or less), there are thousands of copies per cell, and they can be amplified. This kind of DNA can be extracted even from skeletal remains and has been used, for example, in identifying the remains of armed forces personnel from conflicts as far back as World War II.[14] Because of the way it is inherited, mtDNA from remains must be compared with samples obtained from maternal relatives. Therefore, it cannot be used to distinguish among maternally related persons. Also, mtDNA is not as variable as STRs and VNTRs, and it is therefore not as powerful a tool for making positive identifications. It also takes much longer to analyze than STRs.

Some other nuclear DNA markers, such as DQA and Polymarker, are also used to aid in identification. Those consist of simpler DNA sequences than STRs or VNTRs. They can be amplified and require only small amounts of DNA, but they are less variable than STRs or VNTRs, and some of the loci used are closely linked to genes or are genes themselves. However, they can be processed very rapidly and are often used to determine quickly whether a potential source of DNA should be eliminated or

---

[13] Twelve STR loci provide about the same power to identify as five VNTR loci for most populations (Dennis Reeder, National Institute of Standards and Technology, conversation with the author, 9 June 2000). The current standard set of STR loci established by the Federal Bureau of Investigation for use in law enforcement contains 13 loci.

[14] Armed Forces DNA Identification Laboratory, "AFCIL...about us...mtDNA," [http://www.afip.org/oafme/dna/ mtdna.htm], 22 October 1999.

investigated further using more sensitive marker systems. They are also used extensively in paternity cases.

Comparison

Once DNA from the samples is characterized, the resulting profiles are compared. If one or more alleles differ in the two samples, they are said not to match. In that case, if the analysis was performed correctly, the samples did not have the same origin. In the case of a criminal suspect, that means that the suspect did not produce the DNA found in the evidence. In a paternity case, it means that the putative father was not the biological father. If an attempt is being made to identify remains using mtDNA, it means that the person whose remains were typed is not related to the supposed material relatives. This use of DNA as a means of exclusion is a powerful and important use, particularly in the criminal justice system. A common estimate is that one-quarter of named suspects are excluded in cases where DNA evidence is used.[15] Also, in the past few years, more than 60 people convicted of violent crimes in the United States have been subsequently exonerated as a result of DNA evidence.[16]

If the profiles match – that is, if they are identical at every locus – then they could have come from the same source. Alternatively, the source could be someone else who has an identical profile for the markers that were examined. The way such a match is treated in DNA evidence has usually been different than for other sources of identifying information, such as fingerprints. In the latter, a match has usually been considered either a positive identification or inconclusive – for example, either the suspect left the fingerprints or could not be ruled out – depending on the quality of the print. For DNA, in contrast, the science of population genetics provides in many cases a way of estimating quantitatively the chances that the DNA could have come from another source. The chances of such a coincidental

---

[15] Louis J. Freeh, *Ensuring Public Safety and National Security Under the Rule of Law: A Report to the American People on the Work of the FBI 1993 – 1998*, Federal Bureau of Investigation, 2000, 36, available at [http://www.fbi.gov/library5-year/5YR_report_.PDF].

[16] National Commission on the Future of DNA Evidence, *Postconviction DNA Testing: Recommendations for Handling Requests*, National Institute of Justice. NCJ 177626 (September 1999), 2, available at [http://www.ojp.usdoj.gov/jij/pubs-sum/177626.htm].

match depend on both the number of markers used and the variability exhibited by those markers. Therefore, results of DNA analysis have usually been given in terms of the probability that such a match could be coincidental rather than a conclusion about identity.[17]

Calculation

For several years, there was controversy about how best to perform calculations to estimate probabilities in DNA identification, but that issue is now largely, although not completely, settled. The specific procedures can be complex and will vary depending on the circumstances and the system used. However, there are two basic steps:

The population frequency of each allele in the profile – that is, the percentage of people who have that allele in the population examined – is identified. In most cases, those frequencies are estimates drawn from extensive data banks such as those compiled by the FBI.[18] Subpopulations within a country such as the United States vary in the frequencies of different alleles, and therefore comparisons may be made to data from the most relevant subpopulation, usually a racial or linguistic group, or, if it is not known what group the source of DNA belonged to (as is often the case with DNA from crime scenes), from two or more subpopulations.

The frequencies are multiplied together, with the aid of appropriate mathematical formulas, to produce an estimated probability that someone drawn at random from the population would have that profile. If enough loci are used, those probabilities can be very small – on the order of one chance in billions or even trillions – even though the frequency of any given allele is likely to be on the order of 1-10%.

In some cases, probability calculations may not be appropriate or useful. For some loci, the frequencies or alleles in the population as a whole might not be known, or there might be too few loci or too few alleles at a locus to yield useful probability estimates. In such a case, a match means that a putative source cannot be excluded, but there might be many other potential

---

[17] However, those distinctions between interpretation of fingerprint and DNA analysis are beginning to blur (see section on interpretation below).

[18] See, for example, Federal Bureau of Investigation, *VNTR Population Data: A Worldwide Survey* (r volumes), (Quantico, VA: FBI Academy, 1993). The data are drawn from anonymized samples from blood banks or other sources. They should not be confused with the databanks housing DNA profiles of convicted criminals, which are discussed below.

sources. Or the particular case might not require a calculation. For example, if the questions is which of two men fathered a child, no calculation is necessary if the profile of one yields a match and the other does not. Or, in a case of identification of remains with mtDNA, it might be known that a soldier came from one of four families. If the maternal mtDNA profile of only one of the four yields a match, then the soldier came from that family. However, if more than one source produces a match in either of those two examples, then DNA evidence cannot resolve the question unless more loci can be examined. Another situation that can present problems for making useful calculations is where DNA from more than one person is in the sample. In such mixed samples, if the DNA contributed by different people cannot be separated,[19] then it might only be possible to determine if someone can be excluded.

Interpretation

There are two essential questions involved in interpreting the results of a DNA identification: Did the DNA come from the person (or family) who is thought to be its source, and what is the significance of the answer for the case at hand?

The probability calculation, when performed, is used to help answer the first question. If the probability estimate is low enough, the expert who provides it may declare a positive identification – that the person in question was in fact the source of the DNA.[20] However, the questions of what

---

[19] For example, if the DNA comes from different kinds of tissues or fluids, as in a vaginal swab from a sexual assault, it is often possible to separate the male and female DNA. However, if DNA from more than one male is present, separating those is often not possible.

[20] For example, in 1997, FBI experts switched from simply providing probability estimates to stating in addition that a person whose profile matches a sample is the source of the sample, provided that the calculated match probability is less than about 1 in 260 billion (Freeh, *Ensuring Public Safety*, 35; Jennifer Smith, Laboratory Director, DNA Unit 1, Federal Bureau of Investigation, "Comments regarding R&D Report," *Proceedings, National Commission on the Future of DNA Evidence*, 9 April 2000, [http://www.ojp.usdoj.gov/jij/dnamtgtrans9/trans-e.html]). For comparison, that probability is about 1/50 the chance that a person drawn at random from the entire world population would have that profile. The original scientific work that provided the basis for the use of fingerprints in identification established that the probability of a second person having the same

probability level (or other criterion) is required to ensure a positive DNA identification is not yet settled, and in many cases, experts may be reluctant to make such a declaration, preferring to provide simply the probability estimate for the jury or other trier of fact to interpret. That is in contrast to the situation with fingerprints, which are accepted as unique (even in identical twins, unlike DNA) but for which probabilities are not calculated. Fingerprints have been used effectively for much longer than DNA, so little question remains about how they can provide positive identification. In addition, they are not as amenable to statistical analysis as is DNA evidence, although that is beginning to change as automated fingerprint analysis systems are developed and refined. However, with DNA, triers of fact may interpret a very low probability estimate as a positive identification, provided that there are no significant questions about how the evidence was handled, the quality of the laboratory analysis, or special circumstances of the case.

Once a positive identification has been made (or found very likely), its significance must be determined. That would seem straightforward but is not always. For example, in a rape case involving DNA evidence, if the probability of a coincidental match is very small, that would be strong evidence of a sexual encounter but would not of itself be proof of guilt, since the encounter might have been consensual. However unlikely, it is also possible, for example, that there was a laboratory error or even that blood or other sources of DNA might have been planted by someone wishing to frame a suspect. for those and other reasons, a match probability in a criminal case should not be interpreted as a probability of guilt.[21] However, it does provide

---

fingerprint pattern on a given digit was about 1/40 the reciprocal of the world population at the time – National Research Council, *The Evaluation of Forensic DNA Evidence*, (Washington, DC; National Academy Press, 1997), 57. The average match probability yielded by using 12 of the 13 core STR markers used by the FBI is about 1 in 700 billion (James F. Crow, "Research and Development Working Group Report," *Proceedings, National Commission on the Future of DNA Evidence*, 28 February 1999, [http://www.ojp.usdoj.gov/jij/dnamtgtrans4/trans-c.html]). Nevertheless, many forensic experts prefer to provide probabilities but not state firm conclusions about the source of the DNA.

[21] Such misinterpretations are sometimes called "the prosecutor's fallacy." This can be a surprisingly complex issue, and a technical discussion of it is beyond the scope of this report. For more information, see NRC, *Evaluation of DNA Evidence*, 133, 198; and David H. Kaye and George F. Sensabaugh, Jr., "Reference Guide on DNA Evidence," in *Reference Manual on Scientific Evidence*, 2nd ed. (Washington, DC: Federal Judicial Center, 2000), 539, available at [http://air.fjc.gov/public/fjcweb.nsf/pages/16].

DATABASES

Databases or indexes used in DNA identification are of three basic kinds. One provides the allele frequencies that are used in calculations to estimate profile frequencies and match probabilities. Such population databases are drawn from anonymous samples and are separated or stratified according to the population group (usually based on ethnicity or race) of the donors, since allele frequencies, and therefore match probabilities for different profiles, may differ among such groups. Sources are various, such as blood donors or medical patients.[22]

The second kind contains profiles of persons whose identify is known. One example is databases with STR or VNTR profiles of convicted felons or of victims of unsolved crimes (such as the CODIS database system, discussed below). Another is databases with profiles of missing persons or their biological relatives, such as mtDNA profiles of maternal relatives of armed forces personnel lost in past military conflicts (see below). When a profile is obtained from a relevant sample whose source is not known, the database can be searched to determine if a match, called a *cold hit*, is found. For example, in an increasing number of cases, a suspect is identified when a DNA profile from a crime-scene sample is searched against a database containing profiles of persons convicted of violent crimes or other felonies.

The third kind of database contains profiles of persons whose identity is not known. Samples might come from crime scenes or unidentified remains. When a profile is obtained from a relevant sample whose source is known, the database can be searched for cold hits, as above. For example, a profile obtained from a suspect in another crime can be searched against a forensic database of profiles associated with crimes for which there are no suspects. In 1999, a DNA profile of a male murdered in Florida was found to match

---

[22] Such so-called "convenience samples" might seem unlikely to generate accurate frequencies of the distribution of alleles in the underlying population, but they work surprisingly well (NRC, *Evaluation of DNA Evidence*, 126).

DNA evidence from nine rapes, three in Florida and six in Washington, DC.[23]

FEDERAL AGENCY PROGRAMS AND ACTIVITIES

Federal agencies with significant involvement in DNA identification activities include the Federal Bureau of Investigation (FBI), the National Institute of Justice (NIJ), and the Bureau of Justice Assistance (BJA) in the Department of Justice; the National Institute of Standards and Technology (NIST) in the department of Commerce; and the Armed Forces Institute of Pathology (AFIP), the Army Central Identification laboratory, Hawaii (CILHI), and the Army Criminal Investigation Laboratory (USACIL) in the Department of Defense. Major activities are described below.

Federal Bureau of Investigation

Most forensic DNA evidence is developed and used by local or state law enforcement agencies. However, the FBI provides many important services to those agencies and is responsible for processing DNA evidence for cases under federal civilian jurisdiction.

FBI Laboratory. Major activities of the FBI Laboratory include training of federal, state, local, and foreign law enforcement and crime laboratory personnel; research and development in DNA typing technologies; development of an integrated national DNA database program; and providing expert testimony in the courts.[24] The laboratory was the first public crime laboratory in the United States to perform analysis of forensic DNA evidence, creating its DNA Analysis Unit in 1988. It is currently the only such laboratory performing mtDNA analyses.

The laboratory also administers the Combined DNA Index System. CODIS is a distributed system of local, state, and national DNA databases that are linked electronically, permitting the comparison of profiles stored in

---

[23] Federal Bureau of Investigation, "First 'Cold' Hit Recorded in National DNA Index System!", Press Release, 21 July 1999, [http://www.fbi.gov/pressrm/pressrel/pressrel99/coldhit.htm]; Kathleen Sweeney, "DNA testing links rapes to slain man," *Florida Times Union*, Thursday, 22 July 1999, Sec. A, 1. The index system is discussed below.

[24] See the laboratory Web site at [http://www.fbi.gov/programs/lab/labhome.htm] for more information.

different locations. Begun as a pilot program in 1990, it was authorized in the DNA Identification Act of 1994 (P.L. 103-322). More than 40 states now participate. CODIS has several indexes. One, a convicted offenders index, contains DNA profiles of persons convicted of qualifying crimes. Current law does not specify qualifying federal crimes. However, section 811(b)(2) of the Antiterrorism and Effective Death Penalty Act of 1996 (P.L. 104-132) required that states, to be eligible for grants to improve their capacity to perform forensic DNA analyses and certain other activities,[25] collect DNA samples from persons convicted of sexual felonies. All 50 states now require samples from such persons. Most also collect samples from persons convicted of murder or other violent crimes and several from those convicted of any felony.[26]

Other indexes are a forensic index, which contains profiles of DNA samples taken from crime scenes (especially from cases without any suspects); a population file, which contains information on allele frequencies to be used in calculating match probabilities; and a missing persons index containing profiles from unidentified remains.

The national component of CODIS, called NDIS, the National DNA Indexing System, has been in operation since 1998. Laboratories in 24 states currently contribute DNA profiles to NDIS.[27] While CODIS initially used VNTR markers, they are largely being replaced with the more powerful STRs (see section on sample backlogs below). NDIS uses thirteen core STR markers that have been established as a standard set by the FBI.

DNA Advisory Board. DNA typing is technology intensive. That makes issues of quality control and assurance especially important. To help address such issues, P.L. 103-322 required that the FBI Director establish a DNA Advisory Board (DAB) to recommend quality assurance standards for forensic DNA analysis. Following submission of DAB recommendations,

---

[25] Specifically, the grants are made "to carry out all or part of a program to establish, develop, update, or upgrade...computerized identification systems..., the capability to analyze...DNA..., and automated fingerprint identification systems...," provided that they are compatible with the relevant corresponding FBI systems (Sec. 811(b)(1)). Those State Identification Systems formula grants are administered through the Bureau of Justice Assistance.

[26] Dwight E. Adams, Statement, legislative Hearing on H.R. 2810, the "Violent Offender DNA Identification Act of 1999," H.R. 3087, the "DNA Backlog Elimination Act," and H.R. 3375, the "Convicted Offender DNA Index Systems Support Act"; Subcommittee on Crime, House Committee on the Judiciary, 13 March 2000, [http://www.huse.gov/judiciary/adam0323.htm].

[27] Adams, Hearing Statement.

the director established standards effective October 1, 1998. They replaced standards that had been established by the Technical Working Group on DNA Analysis Methods (TWGDAM), a practitioners' group representing federal, state, and local forensic laboratories and supported by the FBI. As of 1998, most of the publicly funded crime laboratories in the United States followed DAB or TWGDAM standards, and about half were accredited by an official organization.[28] DAB is scheduled to dissolve at the end of 2000, at which time its functions will be transferred to the renamed TWGDAM, now called the Scientific Working Group on DNA Analysis Methods (SWGDAM).

National Institute of Justice

The National Institute of Justice (NIJ), a research agency within the Office of Justice Programs, engages in several kinds of activities related to DNA evidence. The institute supports research to improve speed, reliability, and sensitivity of DNA profiling and to reduce its cost. There are three main activities, administered through the NIJ Office of Science and Technology: the DNA Five Year Research Program, the Forensic DNA Laboratory Improvement Program, and the National Commission on the Future of DNA Evidence. The DNA Five Year Research Program (1999-2003), is awarding $5 million per year to support research aimed at reducing the cost and time of processing DNA samples, developing technologies to enhance the reliability of DNA analysis and perform analyses at crime scenes, and developing standard test materials and new markers.[29]

The Forensic DNA Laboratory Improvement Program was initiated in FY1996 with DNA Identification Grants, authorized in P.L.103-322 (Sec. 210302). Appropriations for the program have grown annually (see table). From FY1996-FY1999, the program awarded grants to state and local governments, up to 75% of the total cost of the project, to develop and improve the abilities of forensic laboratories to analyze DNA evidence. In FY2000 and FY2001, funds were awarded under a new series of grants authorized by the Crime Identification Technology Act of 1998 (P.L.105-

---

[28] Greg W. Steadman, *Survey of DNA Crime Laboratories, 1998*, Bureau of Justice Statistics Special Report NCJ 179104, February 2000, 3, available at [http://www.ojp.usdoj/gov/bjs/abstract/sdnacl98.htm].

[29] National Institute of Justice, *Technology Development Portfolio: Investigative and Forensic Sciences*, [http://www.ojp.usdoj.gov/nij/sciencetech/invest.htm], 16 January 2000.

121), with half allocated by NIJ to the DNA Identification Program and half to the elimination of sample backlogs (see below). That program can fund up to 90% of the total cost of a project.[30]

Appropriations for State and Local DNA Laboratory Support, FY1996-FY2001
(in millions of current dollars)

Year	Amount
FY1996	1.0
FY1997	3.0
FY1998	12.5
FY1999	15.0
FY2000	30.0
FY2001	30.0

Note: FY2000 includes funds for addressing sample backlogs. Source: FY1996, P.L. 104-134; FY1997, 104-208; FY1998, P.L. 105-119; FY1999, P.L. 105-277; FY2000, P.L. 106-113; FY2001, P.L. 106-553.

A 1996 NIJ-funded report[31] led Attorney General Reno to charter, in September 1997, the National Commission on the Future of DNA Evidence (hereinafter called the DNA Commission). This four-year NIJ commission is examining several topics, including the postconviction use of DNA, legal concerns, training and technical assistance, and future technological developments. Its members include representatives from federal, state, and local law enforcement agencies, the judiciary, defense lawyers, and other groups and areas of expertise. Rather than producing a single final report, the commission is developing reports on specific issues and making recommendations on an ongoing basis. In 1998, the commission first

---

[30] Information on NIJ grant programs can be found on the agency's Web site at [http://www.ojp.usdoj.gov/ nij/funding.htm].
[31] Edward Connors and others, *Convicted by Juries, Exonerated by Science: Case Studies in the Use of DNA Evidence to Establish Innocence After Trial,* National Institute of Justice Research Report, NCJ 161258 (June 1996), [http://www.ncjrs.org/pdffiles/dnaevid.pdf].

identified the need for a special effort to address a backlog of hundreds of thousands of DNA samples, taken from convicted persons and from crime scenes, that have not yet been processed (see section on sample backlogs below).[32] A 1999 report[33] recommended procedures for handling postconviction DNA-typing requests.

Bureau of Justice Assistance

The Bureau of Justice Assistance supports state and local criminal justice programs. It administers formula grants, including Byrne grants (42 U.S.C. 3751), which can be used, among other purposes, to develop or improve the DNA-analysis capabilities of forensic laboratories; and State Identification Systems grants, which can be used, among other purposes, to help laboratories develop their capabilities with respect to CODIS.[34]

National Institute of Standards and Technology

The National Institute of Standards and Technology (NIST) has played a major role in the development of standards for DNA profiling, as part of its long-standing role in developing technological standards and measurements generally.[35] The standard reference materials that NIST has produced, both for VNTR and STR analysis, are used by laboratories to test the accuracy of their analyses.[36] They are therefore important components of quality-assurance and control activities. NIT also performs research on new DNA-typing technologies, both through the Biotechnology Division (within

---

[32] Paul Ferrara, "CODIS Backlog Elimination Report," *Proceedings, National Commission on the Future of DNA Evidence*, 8 June 1998, [http://www.ojp.usdoj.gov/nij/dnamtgtrans2/trans-f.html]. Specific actions to eliminate the backlog were later recommended to the Attorney General.

[33] DNA Commission, *Postconviction DNA Testing*.

[34] Information on BJA grant programs can be found on the agency's Web site at [http://www.ojp.usdoj.gov/ BJA/html/fund1.html]. For information on Byrne grants, see also Garrine P. Laney, *Crime Control Assistance Through the Byrne Program*, CRS Report 97-265, 8 August 2000.

[35] For general information on NIST, wee Wendy H. Schacht, *The National Institute of Standards and Technology: An Overview*, CRS Report 95-30, 6 July 2000.

[36] For more information on STRs, see John M. Butler and Dennis J. Reeder, "Short Tandem Repeat DNA Internet Database," [http://www.cstl.nist.gov/biotech/strbase/], 24 May 2000.

Scientific and Technical Research and Services) and the Advanced Technology Program (within Industrial Technology Services). Many of the DNA-forensic activities in which NIST engages are performed in collaboration with other agencies, such as the NIJ and Department of Defense, and with private industry.

Department of Defense

The two major uses of DNA identification by the Department of Defense (DOD) are in criminal investigation (see below) and in the identification of remains of military personnel. To aid in such identification, DOD established in 1988 the Office of the Armed Forces Medical Examiner within the Armed Forces Institute of Pathology,[37] under the Assistant Secretary of Defense for Health Affairs. DNA was first used to identify combat fatalities in 1991 in Operation Desert Storm. At that time, the DNA Registry[38] was formed, consisting of two components. The Armed Forces Repository of Specimen Samples for the Identification of Remains (AFRSSIR) collects and stores DNA samples taken from active duty and reserve personnel.[39] Armed Forces personnel are required to provide DNA samples for deposit in the repository. Currently, the repository holds more than 3 million specimens. When a casualty occurs that requires DNA identification, the Armed Forces DNA Identification laboratory (AFDIL) processes relevant samples to produce nuclear (STR and other PCR-based systems) or mtDNA profiles. AFDIL also performs analyses of samples in other selected cases.[40] Two examples of the latter are assisting the FBI in identifying remains after the fire at the Branch Davidian compound in Waco,

---

[37] See Department of Defense, "Armed Forces Institute of Pathology (AFIP)," DOD Directive 5154.24, 28 October 1996, available at [http://web7.whs.osd.mil/pdf/3515424p.pdf].

[38] See Department of Defense DNA Registry, "Welcome to...," [http://www.afip.org/oafme/dna/history.htm], 22 October 1999.

[39] The target date for completion of collection from reserve personnel is December 2002 (AFRSSIR, "Repository History," [http://www.afip.org/oafme/dna/History.htm], accessed 27 June 2000). Specimens may be retained for up to 50 years. However, personnel may request destruction of specimens once they have completed their service.

[40] For guidelines, see "AFDIL...DNA Services," [http://www.afip.org/oafme/dna/outsidedna/htm], 22 October 1999.

Texas, in 1993, and assisting the National Transportation Safety Board in identifying passengers who died in the crash of TWA Flight 800 in 1996.

Another DOD unit involved in DNA identification of remains is the United States Army Central Identification laboratory, Hawaii (CILHI).[41] The laboratory recovers and identifies remains of military personnel lost in past conflicts and unaccounted for. AFDIL performs mtDNA analysis on the recovered remains. AFDIL maintains a database of mtDNA profiles from maternal relatives who volunteer to provide samples, for matching against profiles from remains. As of Jun 1999, 154 matches had been obtained (including 112 from Vietnam and 34 from World War II). The most prominent was the identification of First Lieutenant Michael J. Blassie, USAF, whose remains had been interred in 1984 as the Vietnam Unknown in the Tomb of the Unknowns in Arlington National Cemetery. Lt. Blassie had been lost in 1972 in Vietnam. Samples of mtDNA from material relatives in seven families involved in the investigation were compared with mtDNA from a bone fragment taken from the tomb, and the samples from the Blassie family provided a very close match.

The United States Army Criminal Investigation Laboratory (USACIL) performs DNA analysis for criminal investigative agencies within the Department of Defense. The laboratory analyzes approximately 500 cases per year and recently converted from VNTR to STR analysis using the 13 core loci. USACIL participates in CODIS, providing profiles for NDIS of evidentiary samples for specific cases and searching for matches in cases under investigation, where appropriate. However, the armed forces do not currently collect samples from convicted offenders (see the section below on issues). USACIL works only on cases with a military connection.[42]

Other Agencies

Three other federal agencies support research that has contributed to the scientific basis for advances in DNA identification. The Office of Biological and Environmental Research, in the Department of Energy, and the National Institutes of Health, in the Department of Health and Human Services, are the lead agencies for the Human Genome Project. They also support research on ethical, legal, and social aspects of DNA identification and other

---

[41] See "The United States Army Central Identification Laboratory, Hawaii," [http://www.cilhi.army.mil/], 19 June 2000.

applications of advances in genomics.[43] The National Science Foundation, an independent agency, supports relevant basic research in molecular biology and in the social sciences at universities and other research institutions.[44]

RELEVANT PUBLIC LAWS

When DNA evidence first became available in the United States, questions often arose about the quality of analyses and the absence of widely accepted standards.[45] Also, the typing of specimens was expensive,[46] and its availability to many state and local law enforcement agencies was therefore uneven. The DNA Identification Act of 1994, a subtitle of the Violent Crime Control and Law Enforcement Act of 1994 (P.L. 103-322), addressed quality control and privacy issues. It authorized the DNA Identification Grants program administered by NIJ (see above). The law authorized appropriations for the program through FY2000. It also authorized use of Drug Control and System Improvement Grants for similar purposes (42 U.S.C. 3751; those grants are part of the Edward Byrne Memorial State and Local Law Enforcement Assistance Programs, or Byrne grants). The DNA Identification Act required that forensic laboratories receiving the grants follow specified quality assurance and privacy provisions. Recipients are to meet current quality-assurance standards, as specified by the FBI director, and undergo regular proficiency testing in DNA analysis. The use of DNA samples analyzed by recipients are restricted to use in law enforcement, judicial

---

[42] This description is based on information provided by Larry Chelko, Director, USACIL, email communication with the author, 25 August 2000.
[43] Details can be found at the program Web sites – for DOE, see [http://www.ornl.gov/hgmis/elsi/elsi.html], and for NIH, see [http://www.nhgri.nig.gov/About_NHGRI/Der/Elsi].
[44] For general descriptions of research programs in these agencies, see the following CRS reports: Richard E. Rowberg, *Department of Energy Research and Development Budget for FY2001: Description and Analysis*, CRS. Report RL30445, 12 September 2000; Pamela Wolfe Smith, *The National Institutes of Health: An Overview* CRS Report 95-96, 15 September 2000; Christine M. Matthews, *U.S. National Science Foundation: An Overview*, CRS Report 95-307, 20 September 2000.
[45] National Research Council, *DNA Technology in Forensic Science*, (Washington, DC: National Academy Press, 1992), 97-110.
[46] Ibid., 153-154.

proceedings, and criminal defense. However, anonymized samples can also be used in population databases, research, and quality control activities.

The act also provided for the establishment of the FBI's DNA Advisory Board, to recommend quality-assurance and proficiency-testing standards to the director (Sec. 210303), and required that FBI personnel engaging in DNA analysis undergo regular proficiency testing (Sec. 210305). It also authorized the establishment of CODIS indexes containing profiles of persons convicted of crimes and samples recovered from crime scenes or unidentified remains (Sec. 210304). The Consolidated Appropriations Act of 2000 (P.L. 106-113) additionally provided for an index of profiles from "samples voluntarily contributed from relatives of missing persons" (Sec. 120).

The Antiterrorism and Effective Death Penalty Act of 1996 (P.L.104-132) authorized the application of CODIS to federal crimes and those committed in the District of Columbia (Sec. 811(a)(2)). It also authorized grants to state and local government for participation in CODIS. To be eligible, states must collect DNA samples from persons convicted of felony sex crimes (see above). Also, the National Institutes of Health Revitalization Act of 1993 (P.L.103-43) established as one of the purposes of the National Human Genome Research Institute "reviewing and funding proposals to address the ethical and legal issues associated with the genome project."

The Crime Identification Technology Act of 1998 (P.L.105-521, 112 Stat. 1871) established the State Grant program for Criminal Justice Identification, Information, and Communication. Grants can be awarded for a broad range of activities to, among other things, improve state capabilities in crime identification and promote compatibility and integration among local, state, and federal identification systems, and including accreditation and certification programs relating to DNA analysis. Funding is authorized through FY2003.

CURRENT AND EMERGING ISSUES

Some of the issues discussed below, particularly those related to law enforcement, were the subject of legislation in the 106th Congress.

Law Enforcement and Criminal Justice

Sample Backlogs. DNA samples are now collected in all 50 states from persons convicted of certain crimes. Also, DNA evidence is routinely gathered from crime scenes and victims in cases of rape, murder, and other violent crimes, As DNA technology has improved and states have increased its scope in criminal justice activities (see next section), the workload in forensic laboratories has increased. For example, from 1996 to 1997, casework increased 40%, from a total of about 15,000 to 21,000, and convicted-offender samples increased more than 60%, from 72,000 to 116,000.[47] Given limited resources, forensic laboratories must prioritize the analysis of those and other samples they receive. Therefore, many samples, such as from scenes of crimes for which there are no suspects, and from convicts who are not suspects for additional crimes, are given lower priority. Currently, there is a backlog in the United States of several hundred thousand such samples that have not been analyzed and entered into CODIS databases. That means that profiles from those samples are not available for database searches. Given that "cold hits" have been identified through such searches, the DNA Commission and others have proposed that funding be increased to process that backlog. Also, the $30 million appropriated by Congress in FY2000 for DNA grants included funding for processing backlogged samples.

An additional factor is the conversion of existing profiles from VNTRs to STRs. Some states have not converted to using the core STR markers, and profiles that use other markers cannot be searched against NDIS or CODIS STR records. Conversion requires that a DNA sample be retyped – reanalyzed with STR technology. More than 200,000 existing profiles may need such retyping. Also, there are many "owed" samples – that is, samples that can be taken under existing law but have not been. Those include many paroled or released convicts. The number of such owed samples nationwide may exceed the number currently backlogged.[48]

Failure to process backlogs may have several consequences. Crimes that might be solved with the help of a database match may remain unsolved. That is of particular concern in cases where a perpetrator is likely to perform

---

[47] Steadman, *Survey*, 6.
[48] See "CODIS Offender Database Backlog Reduction Discussion," *Proceedings, National Commission on the Future of DNA Evidence*, 23 November 1998, [http://www.ojp.usdoj.gov/nij/dnamtgtrans3/trans-k.html]

additional crimes, or where a database match would prevent an innocent person from being wrongly suspected or perhaps even charges with the crime. Also, crime-scene samples from unsolved crimes may eventually e destroyed as statutes of limitations expire, permanently eliminating any possibility of typing any DNA evidence.

The size of the backlog makes the question of prioritization particularly important, but it is not straightforward. For example, typing a person's DNA is usually much less expensive than typing DNA from a crime scene, because in the latter case, several samples must usually be processed and, unlike with convicted-offender samples, processing cannot usually be automated with existing technology. That might suggest that the highest priority should be given to typing convicted persons, since many more samples could be processed per dollar invested. However, to make a successful cold hit requires that crime-scene samples also be types, so that they can be compared with the profiles of convicted persons. Also, logistically, it is often easier to obtain a sample from someone newly in custody than from someone who has been released. However, a person while in prison is not a threat to the community, whereas someone who has been released might be; nevertheless, a prisoner might be discovered through DNA analysis to have committed other crimes before having been imprisoned. Finally, solving old crimes with the help of DNA evidence serves justice and might help prevent future crimes, but it might also have negative consequences. For example, reopening a case that is several years old might retraumatize victims or their families who have worked to recover from the effects of the crime.

Additional federal funding to help reduce the backlog could substantially increase the speed with which backlogged samples are processed, easing uncertainties about how best to prioritize the samples and increasing the rate at which crimes are solved. Also, the existence of the backlog could be attributed in part to the success of the DNA Identification Act grant program, and the grant-eligibility requirements in the Antiterrorism and Effective Death Penalty Act of 1996 discussed above. In addition, the processing of backlogs would have benefits across states, especially with respect to "travelling offenders" who commit crimes in more than one state.

Databases. A central issue relating to the kinds of crimes for which DNA is collected from convicted persons for inclusion in a profile database or index. States vary in the crimes for which they collect DNA samples. Qualifying offenses include, at a minimum, felony sex crimes, but several others are included by different states: offenses against children (40 states), murder (36), assault and battery (27), kidnapping (22), robbery (19), burglary (14), and all felonies (6). Also, 24 states collect samples from juveniles convicted of qualifying offenses, most collect retroactively from incarcerated convicts, and some collect from those previously paroled or on probation.[49] In the United Kingdom, the Forensic Science Service, an executive agency of the Home office, maintains a national database with DNA profiles of "suspects charged, reported, cautioned or convicted for a recordable offence," which is any crime punishable by imprisonment, plus certain other specified offenses.[50] Profiles are removed if a suspect is exonerated or acquitted. As of July 2000, the U.K. database held approximately 700,000 profiles and had yielded more than 77,000 matches of suspects to crime scenes since its inception in 1995, with almost 130,000 profiles removed following acquittal.[51]

In determining whether to broaden the range of qualifying crimes, questions might be raised such as the following: What is the cost-effectiveness of profiling those convicted of a particular class of crime? For example, are the resources needed to profile those convicted of nonviolent crimes more effective if spent on profiles or on other aspects of crime solving and prevention?[52] What is the proper balance between using profiles

---

[49] Adams, Hearing Statement. Figures cited are as of December 1999 from an FBI survey of laboratories participating in CODIS. States have continued to pass laws expanding the list of qualifying crimes, so the numbers cited for some categories have since increased.

[50] Among the additional recordable offenses are public drunkenness, taking part in a prohibited assembly, and certain kinds of illegal hunting – Government of Great Britain, *The National Police Records (Recordable Offences) Regulations 2000*, Statutory Instrument 2000 No. 1139, 28 April 2000, available at [http://www.hmso.gov. uk/si/si2000/20001139.htm].

[51] The Forensic Science Service, *Annual Report and Accounts 1999-2000*, 25 July 2000, available at [http://www.forensic.gov.uk/forensic/corporate/annual-_rep/annual_report2000.pdf], 20-21.

[52] The answer to these two questions depends on several factors. One is the frequency with which those who commit nonviolent crimes also commit other crimes that DNA evidence would help to solve. There are few data on this topic so far, but the experience of Virginia might be illustrative. Using a convicted-offender database of approximately 118,000 profiles as of June 2000, Virginia obtained 156 matches of offenders to crimes. The state collects DNA samples from everyone convicted of a felony. Dr. Paul Ferrara, Director of the Virginia Division of Forensic Sciences, has estimated that bout half of those "hits" would not have occurred had the database been limited to violent offenders (personal communication with the author, 28 August 2000). Another factor is the cost of collecting samples and analyzing the DNA for a convicted offender. The DNA

to help protect citizens from crime, on the one hand, and the need to protect the civil liberties and privacy of those who might be subject to profiling, on the other? The power of DNA evidence has led some to call for indexing profiles of all arrestees, or even of all citizens at birth, while others have raised concerns about the effects of such measures on civil liberties.[53]

Postconviction Analysis. A powerful use of DNA evidence is in exonerating the innocent, including in some cases where people have been wrongfully convicted. Several issues are associated with postconviction DNA analysis. Among them are when such procedures are appropriate, and what is the proper role of the federal government.

There are several potential reasons why DNA analysis might not have been done when a case was first prosecuted. One is that the identify of the suspect might not have been an issue at the trial – for example, the involvement of a suspect in a sexual encounter might not have been in question, but rather whether the encounter was consensual. In such a case, DNA evidence would probably not be relevant. Another possibility is that no DNA evidence was found at the time, but turned up later. A third is that there was DNA evidence, but the technology to analyze it was not available when the case was prosecuted. The first use of DNA typing in the United States was in the late 1980s, and it was not widely available until a few years ago.

In some cases, relevant DNA evidence might have been found and analyzed at the time of the original prosecution but yielded inconclusive results because of the limitations of the technology at the time. The much more sensitive STR technology did not become an established standard until the late 1990s, and many states still use the older, less sensitive VNTR markers. STRs or the potentially even more sensitive (but less powerful) mtDNA can provide useful profiles from much smaller or more degraded samples than VNTRs. Consequently, an analysis that was inconclusive with VNTR technology could lead to either a definitive exclusion or, alternatively, a strong match if a more sensitive system is used.

Commission has estimated the latter at approximately $50 per sample with current technology, but it can vary significantly depending on circumstances. A third factor is cost-effectiveness of other methods of crime solving and prevention. These and other factors involved can be difficult to measure and compare accurately.

[53] Rose Marie Arce, "Surveillance and DNA testing are among the latest police weapons. But how will we balance fighting crime and preserving civil rights?" *Newsday*, 30 May 1999, sec. A, 17. See the section on privacy below for further discussion of this issue.

Improvements in DNA technology are likely to continue into the future, potentially making even more samples amenable to typing.

Most states currently do not permit new trials, based on newly discovered evidence, more than three years after conviction.[54] However, DNA evidence, properly handled, is very stable and can often provide useful information even ten years or more after it was initially deposited.[55] This confluence of advances in the technology, the stability of DNA evidence, and its strong and growing exclusionary power raise questions such as whether the time limit should be extended for cases where DNA evidence newly discovered or analyzed can be probative, and whether postconviction legal procedures should be changed to accommodate the particular features presented by DNA evidence.[56]

To date, a few states have passed laws that specifically permit postconviction DNA analysis for convicted persons claiming actual innocence. In considering proposed federal legislation, Congress may consider questions including the following: Should such legislation apply only to crimes under federal jurisdiction, or should it also apply to states? What evidence standard should a petitioner be required to meet for the procedure to be permitted? Should there be a requirement for evidence to be preserved beyond exhaustion of appeals, and if so, for how long should it be preserved? Under what circumstances should elimination samples from victims or other third parties be required? What, if any, accommodation should be made for retyping when new advances are made in DNA technology? Should the government pay for analysis requested by an

---

[54] DNA Commission, *Postconviction DNA Testing*, 9.
[55] In some cases, convicted persons who were actually innocent have served more than ten years before being exonerated by DNA evidence. For examples of those and other cases of postconviction exoneration, see Edward Connors and others, *Convicted by Juries, Exonerated by Science: Case Studies in the Use of DNA Evidence to Establish Innocence After Trial*, National Institute of Justice Report NCJ161258, June 1996.
[56] DNA Commission, *Postconviction DNA Testing*, 10. For example, evidence containing DNA would usually not be newly discovered but would likely already e in the control of the prosecution; however, a DNA analysis might not have been done or might have been inconclusive because of earlier technological limitations. Also, some law enforcement agencies destroy evidence in a case after all appeals are exhausted (Connors, *Convicted by Juries*, 26).

indigent inmate? Should wrongfully convicted persons receive compensation?[57]

Paternity Challenges

As more powerful DNA-typing techniques have become more affordable, their use in paternity analysis has grown. An emerging issue involves cases where men who have legally acknowledged paternity, sometimes for several years, are shown by DNA typing not to be the father of the child. A central question is whether the men in such cases, who may claim not to be responsible for child support since they are not the child's biological father, should nevertheless continue to be held responsible. A concern of child advocates is the potentially negative impacts on children if such challenges are allowed. States have varied in their treatment of this issue.[58]

Future Directions of the Technology

Current research on improving DNA identification is performed or supported mainly by NIST, NIJ, the FBI Laboratory, AFDIL, and private industry. Such research has several broad goals. Improvements in sensitivity of analyses would make useful typing possible from even smaller or more highly degraded samples than at present. That could permit more powerful identification (or exclusion) from DNA in trace evidence from, for example, saliva, tears, and skin cells. Coupled with further improvements in specificity, such as via use of a larger set of markers, it would also increase the ability of DNA evidence to make positive or unique identifications. Even identical twins possess minor genetic differences that could eventually be detected. Reducing the time required to complete typing could lead to more timely following of leads as well as more quickly removing from further consideration those persons excluded by the evidence. As the costs of performing DNA analysis has come down, its use has increased. Further reducing cost would make use of DNA identification more widely available.

---

[57] See Eric A. Fischer, *DNA Evidence: Legislative Initiatives in the 106th Congress*, CRS Report RL30694, 12 January 2001, for discussion of these issues.
[58] See Amy Argetsinger, "Court Opens Door to New Paternity Challenges," *Washington Post*, Thursday, 29 June 2000, sec. A, 1, 19.

Research on automation and miniaturization of the typing process may lead to cost reductions and further improvements in quality control. Conceivably, an automated, portable DNA-typing system could eventually be developed that would permit on-site analysis and identification through comparison against a database via wireless communication.

Such major improvements in the technology will take several years at least to perfect. It is generally believed that STR markers will remain the standard for DNA identification over the next decade, with mtDNA increasingly used to analyze highly degraded samples. Research to develop ways to amplify longer sequences may, however, lead to more use of VNTR or other more variable systems in the near future. Also, the Human Genome Project and related efforts are increasingly identifying very small genetic differences, even at the level of a single base (single nucleotide polymorphisms, or SNPs). Such research may lead to eventual development of better marker systems. In some cases, relevant physical characteristics, such as for eye color, might even be deducible from genetic sequences and could help, for example, in identifying suspects.[59]

There are several challenges raised by the likely future improvements in DNA typing. Improvements in forensic typing will need to be validated by the scientific and law enforcement communities and accepted by the courts before they become widely available for use in cases. Therefore, any given case is likely to involve technologies that are technically sound but not the most recently developed. Furthermore, significant pressures exist to maintain a substantial degree of stability in the systems used. Not only is adopting a new technology costly, but frequent change can lead to longer and more costly proceedings and to uncertainty about the most appropriate approach.[60] One concern raised is that technological advances could lead to a lengthening of the appeals process in cases involving DNA evidence, or a flood of postconviction petitions for typing or retyping in situations where it would not actually be helpful. Such concerns will need to be balanced

---

[59] These and other potential developments are being considered by the DNA Commission and are described on the commission's website at [http://www.ojp.usdoj.gov/nij/dna/welcome.html].

[60] For example, when the first NRC report on DNA evidence proposed a new method of calculating match probabilities (the ceiling principle – NRC, *DNA Technology*, 82-85), considerable controversy was generated in the courts and was not settled until the second NRC report was released (NRC, *Evaluation of DNA Evidence*).

against whatever added ability the advances provide in reversing or avoiding wrongful convictions.

As the power of DNA profiling to identify a person continues to improve, the question arises, can b person be positively or uniquely identified from a DNA profile? FBI experts will currently testify that a person is the source of a DNA sample, provided that the match probability is low enough (see the section on interpretation of DNA evidence above). However, it has not yet been settled generally what probability, or alternatively how many loci, are needed to effectively eliminate the possibility that a match could be coincidental. One complication is that match probabilities do not take into account the possibility of misidentification resulting from errors at the laboratory or in the evidence custody chain. Both experts and the courts have generally agreed that such possibilities are best addressed in other ways.[61]

The stability of DNA evidence makes it potentially useful not only in postconviction typing; it also raises the question of whether statutes of limitations should be extended for crimes in which such evidence is potentially important. That question will likely increase in importance as the number of DNA profiles from "cold cases" grows in databases and indexes such as CODIS. The benefits of using DNA evidence to bring effective prosecutions after a longer period than currently feasible will need to be balanced against factors such as the desire to avoid retraumatizing victims who have recovered from the effects of crimes and the need to prioritize the use of limited law-enforcement resources.[62]

RELATIONSHIP OF DNA IDENTIFICATION OF MEDICAL GENETIC TESTING

Both similarities and differences exist between the use of DNA for identification and for medical genetic tests – with respect to techniques, applications, and the issues raised. The most fundamental similarity is that both rely on genetic differences among people. The most fundamental difference is in the characteristics of the DNA sequences that each currently uses – in particular, variability, functionality, and independence.

---

[61] Those approaches include proficiency testing, laboratory accreditation, and providing opportunities for retyping of evidence by the defense. For a discussion, see NRC, *Evaluation of DNA Evidence*, 85-87, 179-185.
[62] For discussion of this and other legislative issues, see Fischer, *DNA Evidence*.

Variability. A genetic marker used in identification should be highly variable – that is, there should be many alleles, and none of them should be very common. The more variable the markers, the fewer are needed for a positive identification. In contrast, a gene examined in a genetic test is unlikely to be highly variable. That is because genetic tests are most often used in medicine, to diagnose or predict the likelihood of a disease or condition caused by a genetic abnormality, which most people will not have.[63]

Independence refers to whether different loci tend to be inherited together. Two loci that occur close together on a chromosome will usually tend to be inherited together – they will be linked, not independent. Two loci that occur on different chromosomes will usually be inherited independently – they will be unlinked. In genetic testing, only one locus is usually of interest, so linkage is not usually important. In contrast, use of DNA to identify people requires examining several loci, and the mathematics that is used works best if the loci are independent.[64]

Functionality. A sequence is of interest in genetic testing specifically because it is a gene that codes for a particular chemical product. However, in identification, a noncoding sequence or marker is of most interest.[65] That is because the mathematics that is used in identification works best with noncoding loci.[66] Although most loci used in identification are noncoding, it

---

[63] There are other potential used of genetic tests, such as to predict how a patient is likely to respond to a particular drug, but variability at any given locus will usually be low in such cases as well. Also, genetic tests often use techniques other than direct identification of sequences – such as visual examination of chromosomes (karyotypes), or examination of gene products.

[64] In the simplest case, the frequencies of a particular genotype for each locus are simply multiplied together to get an overall likelihood (see section on calculation above). While most medical genetic tests do not currently involve more than one locus, there will likely be an increased focus on multilocus testing as medical genetic technology becomes more sophisticated. However, it is only for identification that independence of the loci is an advantage.

[65] See section on why DNA can be used in identification at the beginning of this report.

[66] For nonfunctional loci the effects of natural selection, which are difficult to quantify, do not need to be taken into account when calculating the likelihood that someone will have a particular combination of alleles; the probability can be calculated directly from the frequencies of those alleles in a population (if certain other assumptions apply). For example, in the simplest case, if the frequency, x, of a particular allele is 20%, then x^2, or 1%, of the population will have only that allele.

is possible that functions for at least some will be discovered in the future. Furthermore, some, in particular STRs, are thought to be linked to coding loci that may be implicated in genetic diseases or conditions.[67]

Regulation and accreditation of laboratories performing medical genetic tests and DNA identification are accomplished through different mechanisms. Clinical laboratories, which may perform medical genetic tests, are regulated and must be certified by the U.S. Department of Health and Human Services through the provisions of the Clinical Laboratory Improvement Amendments of 1988, as amended (P.L. 100-578). Standards are developed by the Health Care Finance Administration and the Centers for Disease Control and Prevention. Medical research laboratories, if they are supported by federal funds or are otherwise subject to regulation, are subject to federal policies relating to the protection of human subjects (45 C.F.R. 46, 21 C.F.R. 50 and 56). Forensic laboratories do not require federal certification, but to be eligible for DNA Identification Grants or Byrne Grants, they must adhere to standards set by the FBI and undergo regular proficiency testing (P.L. 103-322, Sec. 210302). Also, in criminal and civil cases, DNA evidence must pass the scrutiny of the judicial process, where custody-chain and quality-control procedures, as well as other aspects of typing, may be challenged.[68] Consequently, new DNA technologies are likely to be adopted more slowly for forensic use than for medical testing.

Privacy and Discrimination

There is currently no federal law governing genetic privacy and discrimination per se, although Congress has considered several bills addressing such concerns from a medical perspective. The executive branch has also taken some actions, as have several states.[69] The Privacy Act of

---

[67] One, VWA, is actually a noncoding segment of the human von Willebrand factor gene, which is associated with a blood condition (James F. Drow, "Research and Development Working Group Report," *Proceedings, National Commission on the Future of DNA Evidence*, 27 September 1999, [http:/register.aspensys.com/nij/dnamtgtrans7/ trans-k.html]).

[68] For a discussion of those and other legal issues and cases, see NRC, *Evaluation of DNA Evidence*, 166-211.

[69] For discussion of legislative issues and federal and state activities relating to genetic discrimination and medical records privacy, see Nancy Lee Jones, *Genetic Information: Legal Issues Relating to Discrimination and Privacy*, CRS Report RL30006, 2 October 2000; and *Confidentiality*, CRS Issue Brief IB98002, 2 October 2000.

1974 (5 U.S.C. 552a) places restrictions on agencies with respect to the disclosure of personally identifiable information in their possession, including any "identifying particular assigned to the individual, such as a finger or voice print or a photograph." However, it applies only to federal agencies. Executive Order 13145 prohibits genetic discrimination against executive branch employees; it applies to medical genetic tests and does not cover the use of DNA in identification per se. Other federal laws and guidelines provide privacy protections for certain other kinds of personal information relating to health and medical research.[70]

Current federal and state laws also provide safeguards against the misuse of DNA profiles collected in law enforcement. Specifically, the DNA Identification Act of 1994 (P.L. 103-322) required grantees to certify that DNA samples and analyses "be made available only –

(A) to criminal justice agencies for law enforcement identification purposes;
(B) in judicial proceedings, if otherwise admissible pursuant to applicable statutes or rules;
(C) for criminal defense purposes, to a defendant, who shall have access to samples and analyses performed in connection with the case in which the defendant is charged; or
(D) if personally identifiable information is removed, for a population statistics database, for identification research and protocol development purposes, or for quality control purposes…

The act also applies those privacy requirements to federal, state, and local participants in CODIS. However, state laws very with respect to how such samples can be used. Some disagreement exists over whether state protections are adequate.[71]

Samples deposited in the Armed Forces Repository of Specimen Samples for the Identification of Remains are limited to the following uses: "Identification of human remains;…[i]nternal quality assurance activities…; [a] purpose for which the donor… (or surviving next-of-kin) provides

---

[70] See Redhead, *Medical Records Confidentiality*, 4-8.
[71] For two different views, see Adams, "Hearing Statement," and Barry Steinhardt, Statement, Legislative Hearing on H.R. 2810, the "Violent Offender DNA Identification Act of 1999," H.R. 3087, the "DNA Backlog Elimination Act," and H.R. 3375, the "Convicted Offender DNA Index Systems Support Act"; Subcommittee on Crime, House Committee on the Judiciary, 13 March 2000, [http://www.house.gov/judiciary/stei0323.htm].

consent;' or, when specifically authorized, criminal procedures for which '[n]o reasonable alternative means for obtaining a specimen for DNA profile analysis is available..." (DODD 5154.24, Sec. 3.5).

Since most genetic markers currently used in DNA identification are noncoding, the privacy and discrimination issues raised are somewhat different than with medical genetic testing. For example, knowing someone's DNA profile for the 13 core STR loci can provide information about paternity but provides no information at this time about physical traits such as a propensity to a particular genetic disease.[72] However, the issues may begin to converge as new advances in genomics are developed and applied, or if current identification technologies are applied in the context of genetic testing. For example, in some cases clinical research laboratories have reportedly used STR typing of samples as an added protection against the possibility of potential mislabeling.

More generally, as DNA identification becomes more sophisticated, its potential applications are likely to broaden, potentially increasing privacy concerns. For example, it is already possible for parents to purchase kits for obtaining DNA samples from their children and to have profiles developed from those samples and placed in a database to be used potentially if the children become missing. Such private-sector practices are not covered by federal laws and judicial rulings that provide privacy or other protections against misuse or abuse of the information.

Government agencies in other countries have also become involved in DNA-identification activities that would likely be limited to the private sector in the United States. Britain's Forensic Science Service (FSS) is an executive agency of the British Government but is permitted to operate as a nonprofit corporation that offers services not only to the government but also to the public. Among its services to corporations is the development of DNA profiles of employees who might be at risk of being kidnapped. The profiles could then be compared to any biological material provided by kidnapers. FSS also provides paternity-analysis services to the public.[73] The privacy of genetic information obtained or used in such services would presumably be protected by a European Union directive on privacy of personal data.[74]

---

[72] It is, however, possible that some relationships will be discovered in the future, as the functions of human DNA sequences become better understood.

[73] See the FSS website, [http://www.forensic.gov.uk/forensic/entry.htm].

[74] Directive 95/46/EC of the European Parliament and of the Council of 24 October 1995 on the protection of individuals with regard to the processing of personal data and on the free movement of such data, available at [http://europa.eu.int/eur-lex/en/lif/dat/1995/en_395L0046.html].

Such broadening applications may raise concerns about "function creep,"[75] the gradual widening of an application to uses not originally intended. One example often given is the slowly broadening range of uses over the years of Social Security numbers. The identifying power of DNA, the decreasing cost of typing, and the increasing ability to obtain a useful sample without drawing blood, make DNA potentially attractive for a wide range of uses requiring verification of identity.[76]

As long as DNA typing uses noncoding loci, privacy issues arising from its use in identification should remain limited. However, three potential issues might deserve particular attention as the use of the technology increases. First, as genomic research leads to increasingly sophisticated technologies for detecting genetic differences, it may become possible to use coding loci (genes) to provide identification. Use of coding DNA for identification could raise issues of privacy and discrimination similar to those that have raised concerns with respect to medical testing – if, for example, such information became publicly available during a judicial proceeding.

Second, DNA samples obtained from a person – and in many cases from crime-scene evidence, remains, or other sources – contain the person's entire genetic code, not just the profile information. Therefore, the disposition of the samples themselves, after profiling, is potentially an issue. That is especially a potential concern with respect to private-sector activities where disposition of profiles or samples is not necessarily regulated by current law. A case involving electronic commerce illustrates the concern. Toysmart.com collected information about customers under a privacy policy that claimed the information would not be shared with third parties. However, when the company filed for bankruptcy, it included the database of customer information among the assets it was selling. The Federal Trade Commission unsuccessfully opposed the sale of the database.[77]

---

[75] Steinhardt, Hearing Statement.
[76] For a general discussion of such issues for biometric technologies, of which DNA typing is one example, see Congressional Research Service, *Biometric Science and Technology for Personal Identification: Devices, Uses, Organizations, and Congressional Interest*," by William C. Boesman, CRS Report RL30084, 8 March 1999.
[77] Matt Richtel, "FTC Moves to Halt Sale of Database at Toysmart," *New York Times*, 11 July 2000, sec. D, 2: "Judge Shelves Plan for Sale of Online Customer Database," *New York Times*, 18 August 2000, sec. C, 2.

Third, a DNA sample and profile contain information not only about the subject, but also about that person's biological relatives. Therefore, consideration of privacy issues related to DNA identification, as with genetic testing in medicine, must take into account potential impacts on family members. That can raise potentially difficult issues, as illustrated by the following hypothetical example. Suppose that a DNA profile from a convicted offender is similar but not identical to that obtained from a crime scene. Is it appropriate based on that information for a sibling of the convicted offender to be arrested as a suspect? Alternatively, suppose that a person is suspected of committing a crime but there is insufficient evidence to make an arrest. Suppose further that the person has a sibling who has a profile in CODIS. Is it appropriate to examine the profile of the sibling to determine how similar it is to the crime-scene evidence? Such examples are likely to arise in real cases as DNA becomes more widely used in identification.[78]

The growing use of DNA as an effective identification tool, and its increasing overlap with aspects of medical genetic testing, are likely to create a range of policy challenges over the next several years. While this report has discussed several current and emerging issues, new ones may well develop as the technology evolves. The biological role of DNA, the information it contains about family members, and other features of the molecule and the technology may make some of those issues, and the appropriate legislative response, especially challenging.

---

[78] See Michelle Hibbert, "DNA Databanks: Law Enforcement's Greatest Surveillance Tool?" *Wake Forest Law Review* 34 (1999): 782-787 for a discussion of this issue and an application to an actual case.

DNA EVIDENCE: LEGISLATIVE INITIATIVES IN THE 106TH CONGRESS

Eric A. Fischer

SUMMARY

DNA evidence is a powerful forensic tool in criminal cases. Its use and capabilities have increased substantially since it was first introduced in the late 1980s. That growth has led to the emergence of the following issues that were considered by the 106th Congress in legislative initiatives: eliminating the nationwide backlog of unanalyzed DNA samples, expanding the kinds of offenders who are profiled, providing opportunities for postconviction testing of DNA evidence, and continuing development of forensic science capabilities.

A DNA profile may provide powerful evidence in many criminal investigations, either to incriminate or exculpate a suspect. DNA evidence is very stable and can be extracted and profiled from a sample many years after being deposited. The technologies used are increasingly sensitive, powerful, fast, and cost-effective. The cost of performing analyses and the time required continue to decline. Those features of the technology are likely to continue to improve over the next decade.

In 1994, Congress enacted the DNA Identification Act, which provided for the establishment by the FBI of a national index, called CODIS, or profiles of DNA from convicted criminals and from crime-scene evidence. A search of the index may match a crime with a known offender or with another crime. All 50 states now require collection of DNA samples from certain categories of offenders, including persons convicted of sexual felonies. However, DNA samples from offenders and crime scenes have accumulated in many states more rapidly than forensic laboratories can process them for entry into CODIS. More than 700,000 convicted-offender samples awaited processing at the end of 1999. In FY2000 and FY2001, Congress appropriated funds to help address the backlogs, and some states have also provided funding. Several bills in the 106th Congress would have provided additional funds; H.R. 4640 was enacted (P.L. 106-546) and authorizes $170 million over four years.

States vary in the types of crimes for which they collect DNA samples for inclusion in databases. Several have broadened the offenses that qualify. Proponents argue that expansion will help solve crimes because offenders often commit more than one kind. Opponents argue that qualifying offenses should be limited only to crimes for which DNA evidence is commonly used. Several bills in the 106th Congress specified qualifying federal offenses for inclusion in CODIS, and P.L. 106-546 includes several crimes against persons and some property crimes.

DNA evidence has helped exonerate more than 60 wrongfully convicted persons. In many cases, DNA technology was not available or not sensitive enough to produce usable results at the time of trial, and legal and other barriers exist to postconviction testing in many instances. Some states have established a statutory right to postconviction DNA testing, and several bills in the 106th Congress also addressed aspects of that issue, although none were enacted. Aspects addressed included the time period during which testing would be permitted, the degree to which evidence must be exculpatory, how long it should be preserved, whether exonerated persons should receive compensation, and the degree to which states would be encouraged or required to provide postconviction testing.

INTRODUCTION

DNA evidence is a powerful forensic tool that can aid investigators in many criminal cases. Its use and capabilities have increased substantially since it was first introduced in the late 1980s. That growth has led to the emergence of the following issues that were considered by the 106th Congress in several legislative initiatives:

- eliminating the nationwide backlog of unanalyzed DNA samples,
- specifying the kinds of DNA profiles that should be included in law-enforcement databases,
- providing opportunities for postconviction testing of DNA evidence, and
- continuing development of forensic science capabilities.

This report discusses those and related issues and the legislation proposed and enacted to address them. It begins by describing provisions in prior federal law and then discusses issues and the legislation proposed, including the enacted DNA Analysis Backlog Elimination Act of 2000 (H.R. 4640, which became P.L. 106-546).

FEATURES OF DNA EVIDENCE

A DNA profile may provide powerful evidence in many criminal investigations, either to incriminate or exculpate a suspect. As with many kinds of forensic evidence, a profile from a sample whose source is not known (but may be suspected) is compared to one whose source is known, usually the suspect. In such a case, if the two profiles do not match, the suspect cannot be the source of the evidence. If the profiles match, the suspect may be the source of the evidence, or the match might be coincidental. The likelihood of a coincidental match depends on how common that profile is among other people. The characteristics of DNA permit an expert to provide an estimate of that likelihood, usually in the form of a probability. If the estimated probability is very small, a jury or judge might reasonably conclude that the suspect is indeed the source of the evidence.

Other key characteristics of DNA evidence are that it is very stable and can be extracted and profiled from a sample many years after being deposited, provided that the sample is stored appropriately; that evidence can be extracted from many kinds of biological tissues, including saliva, hair, tears, and bone fragments; and that the technologies used are increasingly sensitive, powerful, fast, and cost-effective. Usable DNA can now be extracted from very small samples, such as a drop of blood the size of a pinhead; a profile can yield a probability of coincidental match of less than one in billions or even trillions; and the cost of performing analyses and the time required continue to decline. Those features of the technology are likely to continue to improve over the next decade.[1]

DNA evidence also has significant limitations. It is not pertinent and is unlikely to be deposited in many kinds of cases, such as much nonviolent crime. Even for cases where it is present, it might not be relevant if, for example, the identification of the perpetrator is not in questions. There might be more than one victim or perpetrator, in which case the DNA from different persons may be mixed, making analysis much more difficult. Also, the DNA may be contaminated, degraded in storage, improperly collected or handled, or tested inappropriately. Even with those limitations, however, DNA evidence is an extraordinarily and increasingly important forensic tool.

PRIOR FEDERAL LAW

Recognizing the great potential utility of DNA evidence, Congress enacted the DNA Identification Act of 1994 (108 Stat. 2065, hereinafter called the DNA Act) as part of the Violent Crime Control and Law Enforcement Act of 1994 (P.L. 103-322).[2] The DNA Act established the DNA Identification Grants program (42 U.S.C. 3796kk), authorized through FY2000, to help state and local governments develop and improve their ability to analyze DNA evidence, and it authorized use of Drug Control and System Improvement Grants for similar purposes (42 U.S.C. 3751; those grants are part of the Edward Byrne Memorial State and Local Law Enforcement Assistance Programs[3]).

The DNA Act provided for the establishment by the FBI of a national index of profiles (42 U.S.C. 14132). The law authorized inclusion of profiles from convicted criminals, from samples recovered from crime scenes, and from unidentified human remains. However, it did not specify the crimes

---

[1] For a discussion of the technology and how it is used in identification, see CRS Report RL30717, *DNA Identification: Applications and Issues*.

[2] See David L. Teasley, *Crime Control: The Federal Response*, CRS Issue Brief IB90078, for a discussion of this and other crime control measures.

[3] See Garrine P. Laney, CRS Report 97-265, *Crime Control Assistance Through the Byrne Programs*, for a discussion of Byrne grants. Also, see CRS Report RL30717 for more information on federal programs relating to DNA identification.

covered and did not specifically authorize *collection* of DNA from convicted persons. The Consolidated Appropriations Act of 2000 (P.L. 106-113) additionally provided for an index of profiles from "samples voluntarily contributed from relatives of missing persons."

The resulting system of local, state, and national indexes is called CODIS (Combined DNA Index System). The system's national index, maintained by the FBI, is called NDIS (National DNA Indexing System). Law enforcement agencies usually use CODIS in one of two ways. If they have a profile of unknown origin from a crime scene sample, they may search the index for a match with the profile of a convicted offender. If they have a profile from a suspect in a crime, they may search the index for a match with a profile from an unsolved case.

The DNA Act also established a requirement (42 U.S.C. 3753(a)(12), 3796kk-2, 14132(b)) that participating laboratories meet quality-assurance and proficiency-testing standards and permit access to DNA samples and analyses only

(i) to criminal justice agencies for law enforcement identification purposes;
(ii) in judicial proceedings, if otherwise admissible pursuant to applicable statutes or rules;
(iii) for criminal defense purposes, to a defendant, who shall have access to samples and analyses performed in connection with the case in which such defendant is charged; or
(iv) if personally identifiable information is removed, for a population statistics database, for identification research and protocol development purposes, or for quality control purposes.

Section 811 of the Antiterrorism and Effective Death Penalty Act of 1996 (P.L. 104-132, 110 Stat. 1312-1313, hereinafter called the Antiterrorism Act) authorized the expansion of CODIS to "include federal crimes or those committed in the District of Columbia," although it did not specify particular offenses that would quality. The act also authorized the FBI to provide grants to states (including the District of Columbia) to help them ensure that their DNA-typing capabilities were "compatible and integrated" with CODIS and to develop computerized identification systems and automated fingerprint identifications systems that were similarly compatible with FBI systems. To be eligible for any of those grants, a state was required to collect for analysis DNA samples from "each person convicted of a felony of a sexual nature." Eligibility did not, however, specifically require that those samples be analyzed.

Section 102 of the Crime Identification Technology Act of 1998 (P.L. 105-521, 112 Stat. 1871) established the State Grant Program for Criminal Justice Identification, Information, and Communication, authorized through FY2003. Grants can be awarded for a broad range of activities to, among other things, improve state capabilities in crime identification and promote compatibility and integration among local, state, and federal identification systems, and including accreditation and certification programs relating to DNA analysis.

Those laws, in conjunction with other factors, have been very successful in increasing the use of DNA evidence: All 50 states now require collection of DNA samples from sexual felons, as stipulated in the Antiterrorism Act, and many from other categories of offenders, making profiles from those samples available for criminal identification purposes through CODIS. Hundreds of thousands of samples have been collected from convicted offenders nationwide, and CODIS has assisted in hundreds of criminal investigations. Also, over the past five years, Congress has appropriated more than $60 million to help state and local DNA laboratories. According to the Bureau of Justice Statistics, funding requests received from those laboratories have exceeded available appropriations.[4]

LEGISLATIVE ISSUES

The success of DNA evidence and its increasing sophistication have led to the emergence of the four issues listed at the beginning of this report – sample backlogs, expansion of coverage in CODIS, postconviction testing, and support for forensic science. Those issues and legislative proposals that address them are discussed below.

Sample Backlogs

For the past few years, DNA samples have been accumulating in many state and local jurisdictions more rapidly than forensic laboratories can

---

[4] Greg W. Steadman, *Survey of DNA Crime Laboratories, 1998*, Bureau of Justice Statistics Special Report NCJ 179104, February 2000, 2, available at [http://www.ojp.usdoj.gov/bjs/pub/pdf/sdnac198.pdf].

process them for entry into CODIS. The laboratories usually do not have the resources to process all samples quickly, and they must prioritize those they receive, with the highest priority usually being given to cases going to trial and those where a suspect has been identified. In some instances, released offenders have committed additional crimes that might have been prevented had the laboratories been able to process their DNA more quickly.

Kinds of Backlogs. The backlogs consist of hundreds of thousands of samples from convicted offenders and thousands of samples from cases for which there are currently no suspects. That does not include "owed" samples – those that have not yet been collected – of which there may be similar numbers. In addition, as states expand the crimes covered (see below), the backlog may well increase. As of December 1999, only 35,000 of the 750,000 samples collected from offenders nationwide had been reported as profiled using the most up-to-date DNA markers. Nevertheless, since its inception as a pilot program in 1990, CODIS has aided in more than 1,100 investigations nationwide.[5] By comparison, Britain's national forensic DNA database hold approximately 700,000 profiles and has matched crimes to suspects more than 75,000 times since its inception in 1995.[6]

There is also another kind of backlog resulting from improvements in forensic DNA technology. Many thousands of samples must be reanalyzed, because the profiles they yielded, currently in many state and local DNA indexes, are based on an older DNA technology, called VNTR or RFLP technology, and cannot be compared with those created with the newer, STR, technology that has become the NDIS standard.[7] Use of STRs permits

---

[5] Dwight E. Adams, Federal Bureau of Investigation, *Statement*, Legislative Hearing on H.R. 2810, the "Violent Offender DNA Identification Act of 1999," H.R. 3087, the "DNA Backlog Elimination Act," and H.R. 3375, the "Convicted Offender DNA Index Systems Support Act," Subcommittee on Crime, House Committee on the Judiciary, 13 March 2000, [http://www.house.gov/judiciary/adam0323.htm].

[6] The Forensic Science Service, *Annual Report and Accounts 1999-2000*, 25 July 2000, [http://www.forensic.gov.uk/forensic/corporate/annual_rep/annual_report2000.pdf], 20-21.

[7] VNTRs (variable number of tandem repeats) are a kind of genetic marker that varies greatly from person to person and so can be used to help identify individuals. RFLP (restriction fragment length polymorphism) refers to the method by which VNTRs are processed. STRs (short tandem repeats) are genetic markers that are not as variable as VNTRs but have other advantages. They are processed using PCR (polymerase chain reaction) technology. Although DNA technology continues to advance, the current STR standards are expected to remain in place for several years (see National Commission on the Future of DNA Evidence,

faster typing from much smaller amounts of DNA than VNTRs. It is also less expensive, although conversion costs can be high.

Failure to process backlogs may have several consequences. Crimes that might be solved with the help of a database match may remain unsolved. That is of particular concern in cases where a perpetrator is likely to perform additional crimes, or where a wrongly accused person might otherwise be cleared by DNA evidence. Also, crime-scene samples from unsolved crimes may eventually be destroyed, permanently eliminating any possibility of analyzing any DNA evidence.

Cost of Backlog Elimination. The cost of processing backlogs can be difficult to estimate because of a variability in the circumstances involved. The backlog of convicted-offender samples is much larger than the casework backlog. However, convicted-offender samples are much less costly to process; typing[8] can e largely automated and outsourced. Costs may be substantially reduced if samples can be outsourced to private laboratories and analyzed in large batches, but costs may be significantly higher if samples must be processed in small numbers or by government forensic laboratories, for example in states with relatively small backlogs. Casework generally cannot be automated and can cost thousands of dollars per case, whether or not it is outsourced. Such estimates do not include the costs of any new infrastructure that might be required, for example if a laboratory needs to convert from VNTR to STR technology.

A commission established in 1997 by Attorney General Reno has examined the backlog problem and other issues. The National Commission on the Future of DNA Evidence (hereinafter called the DNA Commission) recommended that grants be used to rapidly eliminate the backlog, that a common set of STR markers and quality assurance standards be adopted by laboratories, and that privacy issues be addressed with regard to outsourcing of samples.[9] The DNA Commission estimated that approximately 450,000 convicted-offender samples had yet to be processed at the time of this recommendation, and that 260,000 needed conversion from VNTR to STR

The Future of DNA Testing: Predictions of the Research and Development Working Group, National Institute of Justice, NCJ 183697 (November 2000), available at [http://www.ojp.usdoj.gov/nij/pubs-sum/183697.htm].

[8] Analyzing DNA to produce a profile is often called DNA typing.

[9] National Commission on the Future of DNA Evidence, *Recommendation of the National Commission on the Future of DNA Evidence*, [http://www.ojp.usdoj.gov/nij/dna/codisrc.html], 16 January 2000.

profiles. The commission also estimated that if samples were outsourced, profiling would cost about $50 per sample with current technology.[10]

Combining the figures above yields an estimate of approximately $35 million to eliminate the convicted-offender backlog. However, that is likely to be low because of infrastructure needs and other costs, as well as the variability mentioned above. It also does not take into account owed samples or unprocessed casework. According to the Bureau of Justice Statistics, publicly funded forensic laboratories reported a backlog of 6,800 unprocessed cases for 1997 alone.[11]

Funding Options. In appropriating funds for the Department of Justice for FY2000 (P.L. 107-113) and FY2001 (P.L. 106-553),[12] Congress specified backlog elimination as one use of the $30 million designated each of those years for state and local DNA laboratories. In FY2000, the Office of Justice Programs allocated half of that funding to address the backlogs. Some states with large backlogs – notably Virginia (191,750 convicted-offender samples at the end of 1999[13]), California (132,000), Florida (55,100), and Illinois (15,500) – have also allocated millions of dollars in state funds to address them.

Several bills introduced in the 106th Congress authorized funding specifically to eliminate the backlogs. Those introduced during the first half of the first session provided $30 million to address the convicted-offender backlog (H.R. 2810, S. 254, S. 899, S.903[14]), which had also been the first kind of backlog examined by the DNA Commission. Those introduced later provided from $60 million to $170 million over two or more years to address both the convicted-offender and casework backlogs (H.R. 3087, H.R. 3375, H.R. 4640, H.R. 5000, and S. 3130). One bill, S. 2859, provided $100 million over four years for the casework backlog only.

---

[10] NIJ, through its Five Year DNA program (1999-2003), is awarding $5 million per year to support research with a goal of reducing the cost of processing to $10 per sample over the next four years, in addition to other objectives (National Institute of Justice, *Technology Development Portfolio: Investigative and Forensic Sciences*, [http://www.ojp.usdoj.gov/nij/sciencetech/invest.htm], 16 January 2000).

[11] Steadman, *Survey of DNA Laboratories*, 1.

[12] For a general discussion of Department of Justice appropriations, see Edward Knight, Coordinator, *Appropriations for FY2001: Commerce, Justice, and State, the Judiciary, and Related Agencies*, CRS Report RL30509, 11 January 2001.

[13] Data on backlogs are from an FBI survey cited in Adams, *Statement*.

[14] See the section on legislation below for descriptions of individual bills.

All those bills required that applicants satisfy quality assurance standards. Other conditions included using state-of-the-art typing methods and providing privacy protections by restricting access in a manner similar to that specified in the DNA Act, as described earlier in this report. H.R. 2810, H.R. 3087, H.R. 3375, S. 254, S. 899, S. 903, S. 2859, and S. 3130 required the Department of Justice to develop a plan to eliminate the backlog(s) addressed in the bills. H.R. 4640 and H.R. 5000 required states requesting funds to develop individual plans. H.R. 3375 gave preference to addressing the casework backlogs. H.R. 3375 and S. 3130 also required that all work on convicted-offender backlogs be outsourced to private laboratories. The other bills either did not specify the kind of laboratory (H.R. 2810, H.R. 3087, S. 254, S. 899, S. 903) or explicitly permitted the use of either public or private laboratories (H.R. 4640, H.R. 5000).

The cost of eliminating backlogs depends substantially on economies of scale. In FY2000, grants for backlog elimination were awarded to individual states, which were then each responsible for processing the samples. States with small backlogs would have higher per-sample costs. Those costs could be reduced significantly if samples could be pooled for processing. One way of doing that is through a voucher system, as provided for in H.R. 4640, and H.R. 5000, whereby states send samples to a private laboratory approved by the U.S. Attorney General. That approach can also reduce state administrative costs and provide more uniform quality assurance.

P.L. 106-546. The DNA Analysis Backlog Elimination Act of 2000 (H.R. 4640, hereinafter called the Backlog Elimination Act) was enacted at the end of the 106th Congress. It authorized $45 million in grants over three years to address the convicted offender backlog and $125 million over four years to eliminate casework backlogs. It requires that states receiving grants specify qualifying crimes for inclusion in CODIS and develop individual plans for eliminating the backlogs. It permits the use of private laboratories and vouchers, includes quality-assurance and privacy requirements, and contains other provisions discussed later in this report.

See below for a discussion of hearings and other legislative activity on bills discussed above.

Profiles To Be Included in CODIS

There were two main issues before the 106th Congress with respect to profiles included in convicted-offender databases: the kinds of offenses that should qualify for inclusion, and authorization of sample collection from offenders. Those issues and bills that addressed them are discussed below.

Qualifying offenses. Before enactment of the Backlog Elimination Act, federal law did not specify offenses except as discussed earlier with respect to sexual felonies. States vary in the crimes for which they collect DNA samples for inclusion in databases. Qualifying offenses include, at a minimum, felony sex crimes, but others specified by different states include murder, offenses against children, assault and battery, kidnapping, robbery, and burglary; and some states include all felonies.[15] Many collect samples from juveniles convicted of qualifying offenses, most collect retroactively from incarcerated convicts, and some collect from those previously paroled or on probation. In Britain, samples can be collected from anyone suspected of a "recordable offense" – any crime punishable by imprisonment, plus certain other specified offenses – and their profiles added to the national DNA database; the profile is removed if the person is acquitted.

Several states enacted legislation in 2000 that broadens the offenses that qualify, and several others considered such legislation.[16] One argument often made in favor of such expansion is that offenders often commit more than one kind of crime. For example, burglary may be a precursor to a violent offense such as rape. While no definitive studies appear to have been done to test that view, available evidence does seem to support it. For example, suspects in more serious crimes have sometimes been identified after being typed in conjunction with lesser offenses. Also, an examination of Virginia data through June 2000 yielded the following results: The state DNA database, which contained more than 115,000 profiles of convicted persons at the time, had yielded more than 180 hits (matches between crimes or between persons and crimes) since 1993.[17] Virginia profiles those convicted of any felony offense. About half of the case-to-offender hits identified would have been missed if the database were limited to violent offenders.

---

[15] See Adams, *Statement*, for a summary of qualifying offenses in all 50 states as of March 2000.

[16] States enacting such legislation in 2000 include Arizona, Colorado, Florida, Georgia, Iowa, New Jersey, South Carolina, South Dakota, and West Virginia. Others where such legislation was considered but either failed or is pending include Alaska, California, Connecticut, Hawaii, Kentucky, Mississippi, New York, North Carolina, Ohio, and Washington.

[17] As of December 2000, 20,000 additional profiles and 100 additional hits had been added to the figures cited here (Virginia Division of Forensic Science, "DNA Databank Statistics," [http://www.dcjs.state.va.us/forensic/DNA_2000_graph.htm].

Also, nearly half the violent crimes solved with the help of the database were perpetrated by persons who had previous property-crime convictions.[18]

Some argue that qualifying offenses should be limited only to those, such as violent crimes, for which DNA evidence is directly relevant. One concern is whether broadening the list of qualifying offenses is cost-effective in comparison to other approaches to solving a crime. Whether it is will depend on factors such as the cost of DNA typing and the "hit rate" – how often a person types for a nonviolent offense will be matched to another crime. For example, if a profile cost $50 and the hit rate were one out of 100 profiles, then the cost per hit would be $5,000. Such costs will likely continue to decline as the technology improves. Another concern relates to protection of individual rights and privacy, both of a profiled person and family members. For example, unlike fingerprints, a DNA sample contains much more information than that used in making the identification – it contains a person's entire genetic code, and much of that code will be identical in close blood relatives. A related concern is that specific DNA sequences from markers currently used for profiling might in the future be found to contain additional information, such as an association with genes relating to disease or other conditions. However, the access restrictions that apply to CODIS (42 U.S.C. 14132(b), discussed above) are intended to provide protections against such broader uses.

Several bills introduced in the 106th Congress listed specific qualifying offenses for inclusion in CODIS.

- serious violent felonies (H.R. 2810);
- crimes of violence (H.R. 3375, S. 254, S. 899, S. 903);
- murder, voluntary manslaughter, and other offenses relating to homicide (H.R. 4640, H.R. 5000);
- kidnapping (H.R. 4640, H.R. 5000);
- sexual abuse, sexual exploitation or other abuse of children, transportation for illegal sexual activity (H.R. 4640, H.R. 5000);
- offenses relating to peonage and slavery (H.R. 4640);
- robbery (H.R. 4640);
- burglary (H.R. 2810, H.R. 4640, H.R. 5000);

---

[18] Source: Dr. Paul Ferrara, Director, Virginia Division of Forensic Sciences, communication with author, 28 August 2000. See also House Committee on the Judiciary, *DNA Analysis Backlog Elimination Act of 2000*, 106th Cong., 2nd sess., 2000, H.Rept. 106-900, Part 1, 24, 34. The report also cites similar figures for Florida (Ibid.).

- other felonies as determined by the FBI Director (S.254, S. 899, S. 903);
- all felonies (S. 3130);
- acts of juvenile delinquency that would constitute a crime of violence if committed by an adult (H.R. 3375, S. 254, S. 899, and S. 903);
- acts of juvenile delinquency that would constitute a felony if committed by an adult (S. 3130); and
- attempts or conspiracy to commit offenses covered (H.R. 4640, H. R. 5000).

S.2783 did not specify particular categories of offenses but expanded coverage to permit inclusion of juvenile delinquents. H.R. 3375 and S. 2783 also expanded CODIS to include profiles from samples voluntarily contributed from relatives of missing persons.[19] H.R. 357 specified inclusion in CODIS for members of the armed forces who are convicted of sexual offenses. The House version of H.R. 4205 included offenses committed under the Uniform Code of Military Justice that are equivalent to serious violent felonies. H.R. 4640 also specified certain violent crimes and other felonies committed on American Indian lands.

Before enactment of the Backlog Elimination Act, federal law did not restrict the categories of qualifying offenses, although the lack of specific authority to collect samples (see below) meant that no persons had been profiled in CODIS as a result of a federal conviction. Representatives of the Department of Justice expressed concerns about specifying particular categories of offenses, for reasons similar to those discussed above with respect to state laws, and support for inclusion of offenses committed by juveniles.[20]

Sample collection. The other issue related to sample collection and application of CODIS to federal, military, and District of Columbia offenders, both prisoners and those on supervised release, parole, or probation. While the DNA Act and Antiterrorism Act authorized inclusion of profiles from such persons in CODIS, federal law did not expressly authorize

---

[19] A similar provision was included in The Consolidated Appropriations Act of 2000 (P.L. 106-113).

[20] David G. Boyd, National Institute of Justice, *Statement*, Hearing on H.R. 2810, H.R. 3087, and H.R. 3375 [http://www.house.gov/judiciary/boyd0323.htm];

collection of samples from them. Several bills authorized such collection and inclusion in CODIS for the offenses specified (H.R. 2810, H.R. 3375, H.R. 4640, H.R. 5000, S. 254, S. 899, S. 903, S. 2783, S. 3130). H.R. 357 and H.R. 4205 authorized collection and inclusion for offenders who are members of the armed forces.

Hearings. On March 23, 2000, the Subcommittee on Crime of the House Committee on the Judiciary held a hearing on H.R. 2810, H.R. 3087, and H.R. 3375. Witnesses from the Department of Justice and state forensic laboratories expressed strong support for the objectives of those bills. A representative of the American Civil Liberties Union expressed concerns about protection of privacy, nonforensic use of samples and profiles, and the potential expansion of qualifying offenses.

Legislative Action. H.R. 4640 was introduced on June 12, 2000, and contained provisions similar to several in the three bills that were the subject of the hearing. The bill was marked up by the Subcommittee on Crime on June 15, and by the full committee on July 26. It passed the House under suspension of the rules on October 2. The House-passed version contained several differences from the bill as introduced, including increased funding for elimination of both convicted-offender and casework backlogs, increased flexibility in how funds can be used for backlog elimination, expansion of the list of qualifying offenses, and addition of provisions relating to privacy protection. The bill was passed by the Senate on December 6 with the addition of a sense of Congress amendment on postconviction DNA testing. The amended bill passed the House on December 7 and was signed into law on December 19.

P.L. 106-546. The Backlog Elimination Act provides for collection of DNA samples for inclusion in CODIS from federal, military, and District of Columbia offenders who have committed qualifying crimes. Qualifying federal and military offenses include murder, kidnapping, certain sexual offenses, offenses relating to peonage or slavery, robbery, burglary, those and certain other offenses committed on American Indian lands, and attempts or conspiracy to commit covered offenses.

Robert Raben, Assistant Attorney General, letter to Chairman Hyde, in H.Rept. 106-900, 23-44.

Postconviction DNA Testing

One use of DNA evidence that has gained substantial prominence is to help exonerate a wrongfully convicted person. In criminal investigations where DNA evidence is used, it has been reported to exclude initial suspects in approximately one-quarter of cases.[21] If the DNA profile of a suspect does not match that from an evidence sample, the suspect cannot be the source of the evidence. In many instances, that means that the suspect cannot have perpetrated the crime, even if other evidence, such as eyewitness testimony, is incriminating. For many cases, especially those that were tried before the mid-1990s, DNA technology was not available at the time of the trial. In others, the technology that was available was not sensitive enough to produce usable profiles from the evidence. In more than 60 cases, wrongfully convicted persons have subsequently been exonerated through the application of modern DNA-identification techniques; in some of those cases, the DNA analysis has also aided in the identification of the actual perpetrator.[22] Such wrongful convictions are of particular concern in cases where a sentence of death was imposed, and concerns about some death-penalty cases has tended to amplify the attention paid to the potential importance of postconviction DNA testing. However, as of January 2001 there were no cases where a person had been shown through DNA evidence to have been wrongfully executed.

Difficulties in Obtaining Postconviction Testing. Attorney General Reno established the DNA Commission specifically in response to a 1996 National Institute of Justice report on postconviction testing.[23] In 1999 the commission issued a report on postconviction testing that included recommendations to prosecutors, defense counsel, the judiciary, victim assistance units, and laboratory personnel.[24] The report discussed the

---

[21] Louis J. Freeh, *Ensuring Public Safety and National Security Under the Rule of Law: A Report to the American People on the Work of the FBI 1993-1998*, Federal Bureau of Investigation, 2000, 36, available at [http://www.fbi.gov/library/5-year/5YR_report_.PDF].

[22] Edward Connors and others, *Convicted by Juries, Exonerated by Science: Case Studies in the Use of DNA Evidence to Establish Innocence After Trial*, National Institute of Justice, NCJ161258, June 1996, available at [http://www.ncjrs.org/pdffiles/dnaevid.pdf].

[23] Ibid.

[24] National Commission on the Future of DNA Evidence, *Postconviction DNA Testing: Recommendations for Handling Requests*, National Institute of Justice,

difficult legal issues often raised by postconviction testing, and pointed out the "postconviction requests for testing do not fit well into existing procedural schemes or established constitutional doctrine."[25] However, it did not specifically address possible legislative solutions, but the commission did consider model legislation separately (see below).

Several factors may make postconviction testing difficult in many cases. First, few states permit motions for a new trial, based on newly discovered evidence, more than three years after conviction (which is the current federal limit, F.F. Crim. P. 33), and in most the time period is less than one year. There are several reasons for such limits, among them that the value and reliability of testimony and other evidence often diminishes over time. However, DNA evidence, if properly collected and stored, is very stable and can often be analyzed with probative results many years after it was initially deposited. Many cases of postconviction exoneration have in fact involved tests done several years after the trial. Also, as a result of improvements in the technology, DNA evidence has become and may continue to become more rather than less probative with the passage of time. A second factor is that the evidence containing DNA will often already be in the possession of the government – it is not, therefore, what would normally be considered new evidence. A third factor is that DNA testing of casework samples can be expensive, and many of the prisoners who might seek it are indigent. Fourth, policies on the preservation of evidence vary among jurisdictions, and in some the evidence in a case may be destroyed after appeals are exhausted. In such cases, opportunities for testing would be lost.

State Laws. Some states have established a statutory right to postconviction DNA testing. In 1994, New York amended state law to authorize such testing for DNA evidence secured in connection with the trial if there is a "reasonable probability" that the results of such testing, had they been admitted at the trial, would have led to a verdict more favorable to the defendant (C.P.L. Sec. 440.30(1-a)). However, testing is available only to defendants convicted before January 1, 1996.

Since 1998, Illinois (725 I.L.C.S. 5/116-3) has permitted postconviction testing for evidence secured in relation to the trial but which was not tested because the particular technology requested by the petitioner was not

---

NCJ 177626 (September 1999), available at [http://www.ojp.usdoj.gov/nij/pubs-sum/177626.htm].

[25] Ibid, xiv.

available at that time. The defendant must present a prima facie case[26] that identity was at issue in the trial and "the evidence to be tested has been subject to a chain of custody sufficient to establish that it has not been substituted, tampered with, replaced, or altered in any material aspect." Additional requirements are that "the result of the testing has the scientific potential to produce new, noncumulative evidence materially relevant to the defendant's assertion of actual innocence," and the testing employs a generally accepted scientific method.[27] Illinois separately enacted legislation (725 I.L.C.S. 5/116-4) in June 2000 extending the length of time that the state must retain physical evidence after a conviction. Delaware (S.B. 329) enacted a similar statute, effective September 2000, which, however, provides a time limit on motions of 3 years after conviction. Tennessee (H.B. 2490) enacted a similar statute, effective July 2000, that applies only to capital murder cases.

An Arizona law on postconviction testing (A.R.S. Sec. 13-4240) became effective in July of 2000. It is very similar to a model statute drafted by the DNA Commission. It applies to cases where evidence that is "related to the investigation or prosecution" and that may contain DNA is "in the possession or control of the court of the state," is in a condition that allows DNA testing, and was not previously tested or "was not subjected to the testing that is now requested and that may resolve an issue not previously resolved by the previous testing." Testing is mandatory if a "reasonable probability exists that the petitioner would not have been prosecuted or convicted if exculpatory results had been obtained," and it is discretionary if a reasonable probability exists that either it will produce exculpatory evidence or "the verdict or sentence would have been more favorable" to the petitioner if the results had been available at the trial. In the latter case, the

---

[26] A prima facie case is one that on its own merits is adequate to prevail unless the opposition specifically presents evidence to disprove it (*Oran's Dictionary of the Law*, [http://www.lawoffice.com/pathfind/orans/orans.asp]).

[27] This is known as the general-acceptance standard for scientific evidence, or Frye test (from the 1923 case, *Frye v. United States*, 293 F. 1013, in which the standard was first articulated). The main alternative to Frye is known as the sound-methodology, or Daubert, test (from *Daubert v. Merrell Dow Pharmaceuticals*, 113 S.Ct. 2786), a broader and less restrictive standard, based on the Federal Rules of Evidence, that was prescribed by the U.S. Supreme Court in 1993. In considering a motion for postconviction DNA testing, a court would rely on such standards to determine whether to allow the use of any new DNA technology that might be requested. Nonfederal jurisdictions vary in the standards they use, and the standards are continuing to evolve.

petitioner may be required to pay for the testing. The law also permits appointment of counsel for indigent petitioners. Evidence must be preserved "during the pendency of the proceeding," and sanctions can be imposed for intentional destruction. The law also provides for obtaining "elimination samples" from third parties. In the event that a postconviction test excludes a convicted person as the source of the DNA evidence, elimination samples may be needed to determine if the source was a known third party, such as a consensual sex partner or a codefendant, rather than an unknown perpetrator.[28]

A California law (S.B. 1342) that became effective in September 2000 permits a convicted person who is incarcerated to request DNA testing. It requires testing if the court finds the following: The evidence to be tested is available, in testable condition, has been subject to a sufficient chain of custody, and has not been tested or would yield more "discriminating or probative" results with the testing requested; identity was or should have been at issue in the case; the convicted person makes a prima facie showing that the evidence is material to the identity of the actual perpetrator or accomplice or certain other factors; the results would "raise a reasonable probability" that the verdict or sentence would have been more favorable to the convicted person had the results been available at trial; the testing employs a generally accepted scientific method; and the request is not simply a delaying tactic. The court may also consider evidence that was not introduced at the trial. The law also permits the state to pay for testing and to appoint counsel for indigent petitioners. Biological evidence from a criminal case must be retained while anyone remains incarcerated in connection with the case, unless the government first provides notice and an opportunity to request DNA testing. The law will remain in effect through 2002.

Some other states also enacted legislation in 2000 relating to postconviction testing. For example, a law passed in Oklahoma permits indigent persons convicted of a felony offense to request a DNA test from the Oklahoma Indigent Defense System. Resulting claims of "factual innocence" are then presented to "the appropriate prosecutorial agency...Factual innocence requires the defendant to establish by clear and convincing evidence that no reasonable jury would have found the defendant guilty beyond a reasonable doubt in light of the new evidence" (22 O.S. 1371.1). The law stipulates that persons who are not incarcerated are not required to provide samples, in contrast to the Arizona law's provision on elimination samples. Also, Washington state enacted a law (S.H.B. 2491)

---

[28] DNA Commission, *Postconviction DNA Testing*, 39.

authorizing postconviction DNA testing for convicted persons who are sentenced to life imprisonment or death "if the DNA evidence was not admitted into evidence because it did not meet acceptable scientific standards or the testing technology was not sufficiently developed to test DNA in the case." Requests are submitted to local prosecutors, who review them "based on the likelihood that the DNA evidence would demonstrate innocence on a more probably than not basis." Connecticut (PA 00-80) now permits at any time a motion for a new trial based on DNA evidence that was not "discoverable or available at the time of the original trial."

Current Federal Legislation. There are currently no federal laws that specifically provide for postconviction DNA testing. However, several bills providing for it or addressing related issues were introduced in the 106th Congress. Legislative provisions in those bills address several questions altogether:

- Can previously obtained evidence be submitted to testing?
- Should the chain of custody for the evidence be a factor?
- Should retesting of evidence with newer technology be permitted?
- Must the evidence be potentially exculpatory?
- For what time period should postconviction testing be permitted?
- Should the government be required to preserve evidence that might contain DNA?
- How should testing and counsel be paid for?
- Should exonerated persons receive compensation?
- Should the provisions apply to states?

Those questions and the provisions addressing them are discussed below.

Evidence previously obtained. A potential gap in current legal procedure was identified by the DNA Commission. In many cases, any testing that might be done would be on materials that had been obtained as part of the original investigation, which is arguably not new evidence. Ensuring that a wrongfully convicted person has a fair opportunity to prove actual innocence might require legislation to provide specifically for testing such materials.

Most of the bills addressing postconviction testing applied only to evidence that was previously obtained. The kind of evidence specified varied somewhat. Some applied to evidence that was specifically secured in relation to the trial (H.R. 3233, S. 1700) or to the investigation or prosecution (H.R. 4980, H.R. 5000, S. 3130) that resulted in conviction, while others applied more broadly to evidence that is related to the prosecution (S. 2859) or to the investigation or prosecution (H.R. 4078, H.R. 4167, S. 2690). Those alternatives could be subject to different interpretations by courts.

One bill referred to new postconviction DNA evidence: H.R. 4162 applied only to death penalty cases and provided the opportunity "to produce any exculpatory DNA or similar evidence which was not available to that individual at the time of the trial that resulted in the sentence of death." S. 2463 also applied only to death penalty cases. It did not provide specifically for postconviction testing but rather for the establishment of a National Commission on the Death Penalty. The commission would examine several topics, including "[p]rocedures to ensure that persons sentenced to death have access to forensic evidence and modern testing of such evidence, including DNA testing, when such testing could result in new evidence of innocence."

Retesting. In some cases, DNA typing might not have been performed at all during the original investigation or trial, and in others, it might have been done but proved inconclusive. One issue associated with the possibility of retesting using newer technologies is how useful the results are likely to be. For example, the result of the original test might have been inconclusive because there was too little DNA to produce a usable profile with the technology used. In such a case, a retest with a more sensitive technology might show that the DNA did not come from the person convicted of the crime. If the DNA could have come only from the true perpetrator, such as in many rape cases, then the person convicted could not have committed the crime. Alternatively, the original test might have yielded strong identifying evidence, such as a coincidental-match probability of one in billions. In that case, a new test would be very unlikely to provide results favorable to the defendant. Another possibility would be that the DNA in the evidence did not come from the convicted person but nevertheless was not exculpatory. For example, as tests become more sensitive, it is increasingly possible that DNA from persons unconnected with the crime will be found, as is often the case with fingerprints.

Several bills would have permitted the typing of evidence that was available at the trial but not tested for DNA or that was originally analyzed with older DNA technology. Some limited retesting to situations where the technology was not previously available (H.R. 3233, S. 1700, H.R. 4980, S. 3130). Others provided for retesting where new techniques could "provide a reasonable likelihood of more accurate and probative results" (H.R. 4078,

H.R. 4167, S. 2690). H.R. 5000 required that the evidence not have been subject to the testing that is being requested. S. 2859 required that retesting be able to resolve an issue that previous testing did not. H.R. 3233 required that the testing to be done use a method "generally accepted within the relevant scientific community."

Potential for exculpation. Most public attention has focused on the use of DNA evidence to demonstrate actual innocence of the crime for which a person was convicted because he or she was mistakenly identified, such as through eyewitness testimony. One issue is whether postconviction testing should apply only to such cases or more broadly. For example, had DNA evidence been introduced at trial, it might in some cases have led to a lighter sentence. However, there is also a concern that such broadening could lead to meritless claims that would waste resources.

The bills that were introduced in the 106th Congress took several different approaches to this issue, requiring that test results could potentially produce evidence that

- is new, noncumulative and materially relevant to the assertion of innocence (H.R. 3233, S. 1700);
- is noncumulative, exculpatory, and relevant to the claim of wrongful conviction or sentencing (H.R. 4078, H.R. 4167, S. 2690);
- if favorable, "no reasonable finder of fact would have found the applicant guilty beyond a reasonable doubt," or would result in a mandatory sentence reduction (H.R. 4980); or
- would, assuming exculpatory results, establish innocence of the crime for which the person was convicted or of uncharged conduct in cases where that would lead to a mandatory sentence reduction (H.R. 5000 and S. 3130).

One bill (S. 2859) provided, like the Arizona statute, for both mandatory and discretionary testing. Testing would be mandatory if the court found a reasonable probability that the requester would not have been prosecuted or convicted if the results of the test, had they been available, were exculpatory. It would be discretionary if there were a reasonable probability that the outcome of the prosecution or sentencing would have been more favorable to the requester.

Some bills further required that requests for testing be made to demonstrate actual innocence rather than to delay punishment (S. 2859, H.R.

5000, S. 3130). Also, some required that identity was an issue at the trial that resulted in conviction (H.R. 3233, H.R. 5000, S. 1700, S. 3130).

The requirements placed on the petitioner also varied. Some required a petitioner to present a prima facie showing that identity was at issue (H.R. 3233, H.R. 5000, S. 1700, S. 3130) and that the chain of custody was sufficient (H.R. 3233, S. 1700) or that results, if exculpatory, would establish actual innocence (H.R. 5000, S. 3130). Some required the petitioner to specifically identify the evidence to be tested and to present a theory of defense (H.R. 5000, S. 3130). Some also contained provisions for assessing penalties in response to perjurious applications (H.R. 5000, S. 3130).

Time limits. The stability of DNA means that it can provide usable profiles even after several years, as has been demonstrated in many cases of postconviction exoneration. Rule 33 of the Federal Rules of Criminal procedure currently permits a motion for a new trial, based on newly discovered evidence, within three years of the verdict. A study sponsored by the National Institute of Justice[29] found that for 28 convicted persons who were later exonerated through DNA testing, the average length of time served was almost 7 years. However, as the technology becomes increasingly available and sophisticated over the next few years, the potential utility of providing for postconviction testing long after the original trial may decrease substantially, especially for previously obtained evidence.

Some bills did not specify time limits during which a convicted person may petition for analysis of DNA evidence (H.R. 3233, H.R. 4162, H.R. 4980, S. 1700). Some expressly permitted such a petition at any time (S. 2859) or at any time after conviction (H.R. 4078, H.R. 4167, and S. 2690). Two took a different approach, providing for postconviction testing during the 30 months after becoming law (H.R. 5000, S. 3130).

Chain of custody. The integrity of the custody chain[30] for evidence to be tested is vital to ensuring accurate results. If it is not properly maintained after conviction, the evidence could be compromised. Also, if evidence has not been properly stored, any DNA present might have deteriorated and not produce usable results. Some bills specifically required that the evidence was subject to a sufficient chain of custody (H.R. 3233, H.R. 5000, S. 1700, S. 3130). Others required that evidence be in the actual or constructive possession of the government (H.R. 4078, H.R. 4167, S. 2690) or in the possession (H.R. 5000, S. 3130) or possession or control (S. 2859) of the

---

[29] Connors, *Convicted by Juries*, 12.
[30] The chain of custody of a piece of evidence is the complete history of its possession from the time it was originally received. (*Oran's Dictionary of the Law*, [http://www.lawoffice.com/pathfind/orans/orans.asp]).

Government or the court. One required that evidence be in good enough condition to permit testing (S. 2859). Several also had specific provisions relating to evidence preservation.

Evidence preservation. The stability of DNA evidence, and its demonstrated ability to exonerate a wrongfully convicted person even several years after conviction, raise the question of whether provisions should be made specifically to preserve evidence that might contain DNA. Otherwise, the evidence might not be stored in a way that preserves DNA or it might be destroyed while a convicted person is still incarcerated for the crime. In at least one case,[31] evidence that had been slated for destruction was instead tested and proved exculpatory.

Some bills required that the government preserve evidence that might contain DNA while a convicted person remains incarcerated, unless it first provides notice and an opportunity to request DNA testing (H.R. 4078, H.R. 4167, S. 2690, S. 3859). One required that reasonably necessary steps be taken to preserve such evidence during incarceration (H.R. 4980). Others prohibited destruction for 30 months after enactment of the legislation in cases in which the convicted person is incarcerated and identity was at issue during the trial (H.R. 5000, S. 3130). Some did not explicitly address the issue of evidence preservation (H.R. 3233, H.R. 4162, S. 1700, S. 2463).

Costs. Casework can cost several thousand dollars per case to analyze, and many convicted persons who might request such analyses are indigent. Such persons would not likely be able to pay for testing or to afford counsel. Several bills provided for government payment, for indigent federal convicts, of the costs of DNA tests (H.R. 4078, H.R. 4167, H.R. 4980, H.R. 5000, S. 2690, S. 2859, S. 3130) and provision of counsel (H.R. 4078, H.R. 4167, S. 2690, S. 2859, S. 3130). Some also required states receiving Byrne formula grants to provide counsel in capital cases and provided grants to help provide such defense services (H.R. 4078, H.R. 4167, and S. 2690).

Compensation. According to the DNA Commission, only 14 states and the District of Columbia provide for compensation to wrongfully convicted persons. The maximum award under federal law is $5,000 (28 U.S.C. 2513). Some bills increased the maximum award for unjust conviction and imprisonment to $100,000 if the person was sentenced to death and $50,000 per year for other cases (H.R. 4078, H.R. 4167, and S. 2690). They also required that states requesting federal assistance for the construction of

---

[31] Cited in Connors, *Convicted by Juries*, 49-51.

correctional facilities provide procedures whereby a person wrongfully convicted and sentenced to death could collect damages.

Application to states. Only a few states currently provide specifically for postconviction DNA testing, as discussed above. The adoption of provisions in federal law could provide an impetus for states to implement similar procedures. Also, federal law could include specific guidelines or grant-eligibility requirements to encourage states to adopt such procedures. In addition, some proponents of postconviction DNA testing argue that there are constitutional grounds for making it available in state courts.

Some bills applied only to federal courts and would have amended Title 18 of the U.S. Code, dealing with federal criminal procedures (H.R. 3233, H.R. 4980, S. 1700, H.R. 5000, S. 3130). Others would have amended the federal judicial code in Title 28 (H.R. 4078, H.R. 4167, S. 2690, S. 2859) and contained provisions encouraging states to provide postconviction DNA testing by amending requirements for DNA Identification Grants (42 U.S.C. 2796kk-2); Drug Control and System Improvement Grants (42 U.S.C. 3753(a)(12)), which are Byrne-program block grants; and Public Safety and Community Policing (COPS) Grants (42 U.S.C. 3796dd-1(c)).[32] The revisions required participating states to make postconviction testing available and to preserve biological evidence. One bill (S. 3130) required states, to be eligible for grants to eliminate convicted-offender backlogs (see section on sample backlogs above), to provide for postconviction testing in a manner consistent with the provisions of the bill. Some bills also explicitly prohibited states, on constitutional grounds, from denying access to postconviction DNA testing if there is a reasonable probability that a favorable result could establish that the person was wrongfully convicted or sentenced (H.R. 4078, H.R. 4167, and S. 2690). One bill would have imposed a moratorium on both federal and state executions until postconviction procedures were established that met the standards laid out in the bill (H.R. 4162).

Hearings. Both the Senate Committee on the Judiciary (June 13, 2000) and the House Subcommittee on Crime of the Committee on the Judiciary (June 20) held hearings on postconviction testing. Witnesses at both hearings included state attorneys general, district attorneys, defense lawyers, and persons who had been exonerated by postconviction DNA testing. Concerns expressed by some witnesses about federal legislation on postconviction

---

[32] See Garrine P. Laney, *Crime Control Assistance Through the Byrne programs*, CRS Report 97-265, 8 August 2000; and David L. Teasley and JoAnne O'Bryant, *The Community Oriented Policing Services (COPS) Program: an overview*, CRS Report 97-196, 7 September 2000.

testing included the possibility of prolonging the appeal process unnecessarily, producing additional trauma for victims and their families, interfering with state sovereignty by forcing changes to established state procedures, and the potentially high costs and other impacts of testing and related activities, including preservation of evidence. Some noted that the impacts of such factors will depend on the breadth of the standards that are established for permitting motions for postconviction testing – that abuse and erroneous exoneration is less likely with narrower standards. Other witnesses held that postconviction testing can ensure the integrity of the judicial process without placing undue burdens on it, and that federal legislation is required to ensure that testing is available with appropriate standards in all states.

No bills specifically addressing the issues discussed in this section were enacted in the 106th Congress. However, the Backlog Elimination Act contains a provision indicating the sense of Congress that grants to states for forensic science should be conditioned on the provision of postconviction DNA testing by those states, and that Congress should work with states to ensure that defendants in capital cases have competent counsel.

OTHER ISSUES

Funding. From FY1996-FY1999, Congress appropriated more than $30 million for DNA Identification grants authorized through FY2000 under the DNA Act. The purpose of those discretionary grants was to improve the DNA-analysis capabilities of state and local forensic laboratories.[33] For FY2000 and FY2001, Congress appropriated $30 million each year, under authorization provided by the Crime Identification Technology Act, for the Crime Laboratory Improvement Program (CLIP), to support those activities and general forensic science capabilities of the laboratories, and for backlog elimination grants.[34]

In addition to the backlog elimination funding contained in bills discussed earlier, several bills provided more broadly for federal funding in support of DNA analysis. H.R. 3144, S. 1760, and S. 2783 authorized Law

---

[33] There are approximately 120 publicly funded crime laboratories in the United States.

[34] CLIP provides up to 90% of the cost of a project, and DNA Identification grants up to 75%.

Enforcement Technology grants, under the COPS program,[35] which could be used, among other purposes, for developing and improving state and local DNA-analysis capabilities. H.R. 2340 and S. 1196 established a program of Forensic Sciences Improvement Grants to states to improve their forensic science services, and authorized $768 million over 5 years for those formula grants. S. 9 would have extended authorization of DNA Identification Grants through FY 2002.]

Office of Science and Technology. H.R. 4403 would have established within the Office of Justice Programs a separate Office of Science and Technology, which would assume the functions of the current Office of Science and Technology at the National Institute of Justice. Its duties would include research and development of DNA technologies.

Statutes of limitations. The stability of DNA evidence has led to exoneration in some cases several years after conviction. That same stability also raises the possibility of identifying perpetrators years after a crime has been committed – even after the statute of limitations for a crime has expired. That has led some states to consider extending statutes of limitations for some crimes, and it has led prosecutors in some cases to seek "John Doe" indictments of unknown persons, based on the DNA profiles obtained from crime-scene evidence.[36] The bills discussed in this report did not address this issue, except that H.R. 4640, as introduced, provided that a state plan to address casework backlogs may include cases for which the statute of limitations has expired. That provision was later deleted.

Expungement of DNA Records. Current federal law relating to CODIS does not contain specific provisions providing for (1) the removal of the DNA profiles of a convicted person if the conviction is overturned or (2) the destruction of blood or other DNA samples taken from a convicted person in such a case, or (3) removal of profiles, taken from crime scene evidence, of

---

[35] For a general discussion of this program, see David Teasley and JoAnne O'Bryant, *The Community Oriented Policing Services (COPS) Program: An Overview*, CRS Report 97-196.

[36] California has enacted legislation (AB 1742) that extends the statute of limitations for certain sex crimes from 6 to 10 years. However, it did not become effective until a postconviction testing bill (SB 1342) became law – see section on postconviction testing above. Connecticut (PA 00-80) has extended the statute of limitations to 20 years for sexual assaults for which a DNA profile of the perpetrator is obtained from the evidence. Colorado has enacted legislation (HB 1216) that permits indictment of an unnamed offender on the basis of the person's DNA profile. Delaware (SB 329) has extended the statute of limitations to 10 years for crimes where the prosecution is based on DNA evidence.

persons who are not suspects. State laws vary in their provisions with respect to such expungement.[37] Several of the bills discussed in this report addressed situation (1); they contained provisions for removing DNA identification records and analyses in the event of an overturned conviction or related event (H.R. 2810, H.R. 3375, H.R. 4205, H.R. 4640, H.R. 5000, S. 254,[38] S. 899, S. 903, and S. 3130). Supporters of expungement provisions argue that they are necessary for protection of the individual rights and privacy of innocent persons.[39] Opponents argue that DNA records should not be treated differently than fingerprints, which are normally not subject to expungement, and that existing safeguards make expungement unnecessary to protect privacy and prevent misuse.[40] P.L. 106-546 provides for expungement of records if a conviction is overturned.

LEGISLATION

The following laws, enacted in the 106th Congress, contain provisions relating to DNA evidence:

P.L. 106-113. Departments of Commerce, Justice, and State, the Judiciary, and Related Agencies Appropriations Act, 2000. Designated $30 million for state and local DNA laboratories, under programs authorized by the Crime Identification Technology Act of 1998 (P.L. 105-521). DOJ allocated half of that funding to address backlogs. Signed into law, November 29, 1999.

P.L. 106-553. Departments of Commerce, Justice, and State, the Judiciary, and Related Agencies Appropriations Act, 2001. Designated $30 million for state and local DNA laboratories, under programs authorized by the Crime identification Technology Act of 1998 (P.L. 105-521), to be used for backlog elimination and laboratory improvement. Signed into law, December 21, 2000.

Minnesota (HB 2688) has eliminated the statute of limitations for certain sex crimes where there is physical evidence that can be tested for DNA.

[37] Michelle Hibbert, "DNA Databanks: Law Enforcement's Greatest Surveillance Tool?" *Wake Forest Law Review* 34 (1999): 808-812.

[38] Expungement provisions in S. 254 apply only to juveniles.

[39] Hibbert, "DNA Databanks," 812, 816-817.

[40] Boyd, *Statement*; Raben, letter in H.Rept. 106-900, 38.

P.L. 106-546. DNA Analysis Backlog Elimination Act of 2000 (H.R. 4640 – McCollum). Provides $170 million over four years to assist states in analyzing convicted-offender and casework samples. Expands CODIS to include criminal offenses committed under Federal law, UCMJ, and DC Code. Requires establishment of qualifying offenses, to include kidnapping, offenses relating to homicide or to peonage or slavery, certain sexual offenses, robbery or burglary, certain offenses committed on American Indian Lands, and attempts or conspiracy to commit covered offenses; authorizes collection of samples from those convicted. Specifies privacy protections, adherence to quality-assurance standards, and expungement of records if conviction is overturned. Indicates sense of Congress that states should provide for postconviction DNA testing and competent defense counsel in capital cases. Introduced June 12, 2000; referred to Committees on the Judiciary and Armed Services. Ordered reported, with amendments, by Judiciary, July 26. See H.Rept. 106-900, Part I. Discharged by Armed Services, September 26. Passed House, amended, October 2. Passed Senate, amended, December 6. House agreed to Senate amendment, December 7. Signed by President, December 19, 2000.

The following bills, introduced in the 106th Congress, were not enacted (except H.R. 4205, from which provisions relating to DNA evidence were deleted before enactment).

H.R. 357 (Conyers). Violence Against Women Act of 1999. Required anyone convicted by court-martial of a sexual offense to provide a DNA sample for inclusion in CODIS. Contained other measures to help prevent violence against women. Introduced January 19, 1999; referred to the Committees on the Judiciary, Education and the Workforce, Ways and means, Commerce, Banking and Financial Services, Armed Services, and Government Reform.

H.R. 1501 (McCollum). Consequences for Juvenile Offenders Act of 1999. See S. 254. Introduced April 21, 1999; reported by Crime Subcommittee of Committee on the Judiciary, April 22. Passed House, amended, June 17, 1999. Senate amended, passed, and appointed conferees, July 28, 1999. House appointed conferees, July 30, 1999.

H.R. 2340 (Bishop)/S. 1196 (Coverdell). National Forensic Sciences Improvement Act of 1999. Provided $768 million over 5 years for Forensic

Sciences Improvement Grants, which are formula grants to states to improve their forensic science services. S. 1196 introduced June 9, 1999, H.R. 2340 introduced June 24, 1999; referred to Committee on the Judiciary.

H.R. 2810 (Kennedy). Violent Offender DNA Identification Act of 1999. Required voluntary plan, and provided $30 million over two years, to assist state and local forensic laboratories to eliminate convicted-offender backlog. Expanded CODIS to include criminal offenses committed under Federal law, Uniform Code of Military Justice (UCMJ), and District of Columbia (DC) Code. Required establishment of qualifying criminal offenses, to include serious violent felony or burglary; authorized collection of samples from those convicted. Specified privacy protections and adherence to quality-assurance standards. Introduced Jun3 8, 1999; referred to Committees on the Judiciary and Armed Services. Hearings held by Judiciary Subcommittee on Crime, March 23, 2000.

H.R. 3087 (Weiner). DNA Backlog Elimination Act. Required voluntary plan, and provided $60 million over two years, to assist state and local forensic laboratories to eliminate convicted-offender and casework backlogs. Specified privacy protections and adherence to quality-assurance standards. Introduced October 14, 1999; referred to Committee on the Judiciary. Hearings helf by Judiciary Subcommittee on Crime, March 23, 2000.

H.R. 3144 (Weiner)/S. 1760 (Biden). Providing Reliable Officers, Technology, Education, Community Prosecutors, and Training In Our Neighborhoods Act of 1999 or PROTECTION Act. Authorized use of COPS grants for, among other purposes, enhancing law enforcement access to new technologies, including developing and improving state and local DNA-analysis capabilities. S. 1760 introduced October 21, 1999, H.R. 3144 introduced October 25, 1999; referred to Committee on the Judiciary.

H.R. 3233 (Jackson)/S. 1700 (Durbin). Right to Use Technology in the Hunt for Truth Act or TRUTH Act. Amended federal criminal procedure to allow a court, on a motion by defendant, to order DNA testing of evidence secured in relation to trial but not tested because the technology was not available. Required defendant to present prima facie case that identity was an issue at trial and that the evidence was subject to a sufficient chain of custody. Directed court to allow testing if it determined that results had potential to produce evidence materially relevant to defendant's assertion of innocence, and that testing requested employed a scientific method generally accepted within relevant scientific community. S. 1700 introduced October 6, 1999, H.R. 3233 introduced November 5, 1999; referred to Committee on the Judiciary.

H.R. 3375 (Gilman). Convicted Offender DNA Index System Support Act. Required plan, and provided $79 million over two years. to assist state and local forensic laboratories to eliminate convicted-offender and casework backlogs. Gave preference to states that had developed programs for analyzing samples from cases with no suspects. Required that analysis of convicted-offender samples be performed by private laboratories. Expanded CODIS to include information from relatives of missing persons and to criminal offenses and acts of juvenile offenses; authorized collection of samples from those convicted. Specified privacy protections and adherence to quality-assurance standards. Introduced November 16, 1999; referred to Committees on the Judiciary and Armed Services. Hearings held by Judiciary Subcommittee on Crime, March 23, 2000.

H.R. 4078 (Hastings)/H.R. 4167 (Delahunt)/S. 2690 (Leahy). Innocence Protection Act of 2000. Amended federal judicial code to permit a person convicted in a federal court to apply at any time for DNA testing of evidence related to the investigation or prosecution, in the possession of the government, and either was not tested or could be retested with new technology that will likely provide more accurate and probative results. Directed court to order testing if it determines that results may produce exculpatory evidence relevant to applicant's claim of wrongful conviction or sentencing. Required preservation of relevant biological evidence while person was incarcerated, with exceptions. Provided for government funding of testing and counsel for indigent applicants. Established posttesting procedures. Requires states, to be eligible for DNA Identification or Byrne grants, to provide for postconviction testing, evidence preservation, and competent legal services for indigent persons in capital cases; and prohibited denial by a state of request for postconviction testing, if criteria were met. Provided for compensation for wrongfully convicted persons. Specified privacy protections and adherence to quality-assurance standards. H.R. 4078 introduced March 23, 2000, H.R. 4167 introduced April 4; referred to Committee on the Judiciary. Hearings held by Judiciary Subcommittee on Crime, June 20. S. 2690 introduced June 7, 2000; referred to Committee on the Judiciary (see also S. 2073), introduced February 10, 2000).

H.R. 4162 (Jackson). Accuracy in Judicial Administration Act of 2000. Established moratorium on executions and directed Attorney General to prescribe standards to provide overwhelming confidence that innocent parties would not suffer death penalty, including procedures to assure that a person convicted of capital offense had opportunity to produce exculpatory DNA or similar evidence not available at time of trial. Moratorium would have ended on the later of seven years after enactment or establishment of approved standards and procedures. Introduced April 14, 2000; referred to Committee on the Judiciary (see also H.R. 3623, introduced March 27, 2000).

H.R. 4205 (Spence). Floyd D. Spence National Defense Authorization Act for Fiscal Year 2001. Authorized appropriations for FY 2001 for defense activities of Departments of Defense and Energy, and other purposes. House version expanded CODIS to include offenses committed under UCMJ that were equivalent to serious violent felonies and authorizes collection of DNA samples from offenders. Senate version and enacted bill (H.R. 5408, P.L. 106-398) did not include that provision. Introduced April 6, 2000; referred to Committee on Armed Services; reported with amendments, May 12; passed House May 18. Passes Senate July 13, 2ith amendments, and conferees appointed. House appointed conferees, July 27. Conference report (H.Rept. 106-945) including the substitute (H.R. 5408) approved by House on October 11 and Senate October 12. Signed by President October 30, 2000.

H.R. 4403 (Boehlert). Law Enforcement Science and Technology Act of 2000. Would have established, within Office of Justice Programs of DOJ, an Office of Science and Technology, to carry out programs to improve safety, effectiveness, and access to law-enforcement technology, including DNA; replaced office of same name currently within National Institute of Justice. Provided $1 billion over five years for office and programs. Introduced May 9, 2000; referred to Committee on the Judiciary.

H.R. 4980 (Sensenbrenner). Scientific Certainty in Sentencing Act of 2000. Would have amended federal criminal procedure to allow a court, on a motion by a defendant, to order DNA testing of evidence that was secured in relation to an investigation or prosecution resulting in conviction but was not tested because the technology was not available. Directed the court to order testing if, assuming a favorable result, no reasonable finder of fact would have found the applicant guilty at trial, or there would have been a mandatory reduction in the sentence. Required preservation of relevant biological evidence while the person was incarcerated, with exceptions. Introduced July 26, 2000; referred to Committee on the Judiciary.

H.R. 5000 (McCollum). Criminal Justice Integrity and Law Enforcement Assistance Act. Provided $170 million over four years to assist states in analyzing convicted-offender and casework samples. Expanded CODIS to include criminal offenses committed under Federal law, UCMJ, and DC Code. Required establishment of qualifying offenses, to include kidnapping, offenses relating to homicide, certain sexual offenses, burglary, or attempts or conspiracy to commit such offenses; authorized collection of samples from those convicted. Specified privacy protections and adherence to quality-assurance standards. Amended federal criminal procedure to allow a court, on motion by defendant during the 30 months after enactment, to order DNA testing of evidence secured in relation to investigation or prosecution resulting in conviction but not subject to testing requested. Required defendant to assert innocence, under penalty of perjury; identify evidence to be tested and theory of defense not inconsistent with those previously asserted; and present prima facie case that identity was an issue in trial and that evidence, if exculpatory, would establish innocence or result in reduction in sentence. Directed court to order testing, with exceptions, if it determined that defendant met requirements, evidence was subject to sufficient chain of custody, and motion was timely and was made to demonstrate actual innocence. Required preservation of relevant biological evidence. Provided for government funding of testing for indigent applicants. Established posttesting procedures. Introduced July 27, 2000; referred to Committees on the Judiciary and Armed Services.

S. 9 (Daschle). Safe Schools, Safe Streets, and Secure Borders Act of 1999. Criminal justice bill that included extension of authorization of DNA Identification Grants through FY 2002. Introduced January 19, 1999; referred to the Committee on the Judiciary.

S. 254 (Hatch). Violent and Repeat Juvenile Offender Accountability and Rehabilitation Act of 1999. Juvenile justice bill that included provisions requiring voluntary plan, and providing $30 million over two years, to assist state and local forensic laboratories to eliminate convicted-offender backlog. Expanded CODIS to include criminal offenses and acts of juvenile delinquency committed under Federal law, UCMJ, and the DC Code. Required establishment of qualifying offenses, to include crimes of violence and equivalent juvenile offenses; authorizes collection of samples from those convicted. Specified privacy protections and adherence to quality-assurance standards. Introduced January 20, 1999. Passed Senate, amended, May 20, 1999. Received in House, May 26. Returned to the Senate pursuant to the provisions of H.Res. 249, July 16, 1999.

S. 899 (Hatch). 21st Century Justice Act of 1999. Omnibus crime bill containing provisions relating to DNA evidence similar to those in S. 254. Introduced April 28, 1999; referred to Committee on Judiciary.

S. 903 (Kohl). Violent Offender DNA Identification Act of 1999. Required voluntary plan, and provided $30 million over two years, to assist state and local forensic laboratories to eliminate convicted-offender backlog. Expanded CODIS to include criminal offenses and acts of juvenile delinquency committed under Federal law, UCMJ, and the DC Code. Required establishment of qualifying criminal offenses, to include crimes of violence and equivalent juvenile offenses; authorized collection of samples from those convicted. Specified privacy protections and adherence to quality-assurance standards. Introduced April 28, 1999; referred to Committee on the Judiciary.

S. 2463 (Feingold). National Death Penalty Moratorium Act of 2000. Would have instituted moratorium on imposition of death penalty at federal and state levels until a national commission studied its use, and Congress considered findings. Among issues to be studied were procedures to ensure that persons sentenced to death have access to potentially exonerating forensic evidence, including DNA testing. Introduced April 26, 2000; referred to Committee on the Judiciary.

S. 2783 (Leahy). 21st Century Law Enforcement and Public Safety Act. Omnibus crime bill. Expanded CODIS to include information from relatives of missing persons and to criminal offenses and acts of juvenile delinquency committed under Federal law, the UCMJ, and DC Code. Authorized use of COPS grants for, among other purposes, enhancing law enforcement access to new technologies, including developing and improving state and local DNA-analysis capabilities. Introduced June 26, 2000; referred to Committee on the Judiciary.

S. 2859 (Schumer). DNA Testing Availability Act. Required plan, and provided $100 million over four years, to assist state and local forensic laboratories to eliminate casework backlogs of unsolved crimes. Specified privacy protections and adherence to quality-assurance standards. Amended federal judicial code to permit a person convicted in a federal court to apply at any time for DNA testing of evidence related to the prosecution leading to conviction and in possession or control of government. Directed court to order testing if it determined that results, if exculpatory, would not have led to prosecution of conviction and would likely have provided more accurate and probative results relevant to applicant's claim of wrongfully conviction or sentencing; evidence was in testable condition and was not tested in the way requested; and request was made to demonstrate actual innocence. Court could also order discretionary testing if it might reasonably lead to more favorable outcome for requestor. provided for government funding of testing and counsel for indigent applicants. Required preservation of relevant biological evidence while person is incarcerated, with exceptions. Established posttesting procedures. Required states, to be eligible for DNA Identification or Byrne grants, to provide for postconviction testing and evidence preservation. Introduced July 13, 2000; referred to Committee on the Judiciary.

S. 3130 (Hatch). Criminal Justice Integrity and Law Enforcement Assistance Act. Required plan, and provided $120 million over two years, to assist state and local forensic laboratories to eliminate convicted-offender and casework backlogs. Required that analysis of convicted-offender samples be performed by private laboratories. Expanded CODIS to include information from relatives of missing persons and to criminal offenses and acts of juvenile delinquency committed under Federal law, UCMJ, and DC Code. Required establishment of qualifying offenses, to include felonies and equivalent juvenile offenses; authorized collection of samples from those convicted. Specified privacy protections and adherence to quality-assurance standards. Would have amended federal criminal procedure to allow a court, on motion by defendant during the 30 months after enactment, to order DNA testing of evidence secured in relation to investigation or prosecution resulting in conviction but not subject to testing requested. Required defendant to assert innocence, under penalty of perjury; identify evidence to be tested and theory of defense not inconsistent with those previously asserted; and present prima facie case that identity was an issue in trial and that evidence, if exculpatory, would establish innocence or result in reduction in sentence. Directed court to order testing, with exceptions, if it determined that defendant met requirements, evidence was subject to sufficient chain of custody, and motion was timely and was made to demonstrate actual innocence. Required preservation of relevant biological evidence. Provided for government funding of testing and counsel for indigent applicants. Established posttesting procedures. Introduced September 28, 2000; referred to Committee on the Judiciary.

INDEX

A

AFDIL, 21, 22, 31
AFRSSIR, 21
alleles, 5, 6, 7, 9, 11, 14, 33, 34
Armed Forces, 3, 9, 15, 21, 36
Armed Forces DNA Identification laboratory, 21
Armed Forces Repository of Specimen Samples for the Identification of Remains, 21, 36

B

Bureau of Justice Assistance, 2, 15, 16, 19

C

capital cases, 65, 67, 70, 72
chromosomes, 5, 6, 33
CODIS, 2, 3, 14, 15, 16, 19, 20, 22, 24, 25, 27, 33, 36, 39, 42, 45, 46, 47, 51, 53, 54, 55, 68, 69, 70, 71, 72, 73, 74, 75, 76, 77
coincidental match, 10, 13, 43, 44
cold hit, 14, 26
Combined DNA Index System, 2, 15, 45
conviction, 29, 54, 57, 58, 61, 62, 63, 64, 65, 68, 70, 72, 74, 76, 77
Crime Identification Technology Act, 2, 18, 24, 46, 67, 69
crime scenes, 11, 14, 16, 18, 19, 24, 25, 27, 42, 45

D

death penalty, 61, 73, 75
defendant, 3, 36, 45, 57, 58, 60, 62, 71, 74, 77
Department of Defense, 15, 20, 21, 22
discrimination, 35, 36, 38
DNA Advisory Board, 17, 24
DNA Analysis Backlog Elimination Act, 43, 51, 53, 69
DNA Commission, 19, 25, 28, 29, 31, 49, 50, 56, 58, 59, 61, 65
DNA Evidence, v, 3, 10, 12, 13, 14, 17, 19, 25, 29, 30, 32, 33, 34, 35, 41, 43, 48, 49, 56, 57
DNA Identification Act, 2, 16, 23, 26, 35, 36, 42, 44, 48, 71, 75

DNA Identification Grants, 18, 23, 35, 44, 66, 67, 75
DNA profiles, 11, 16, 27, 32, 35, 37, 43, 68
DNA profiling, 4, 17, 20, 32
DNA technology, 1, 25, 29, 30, 42, 48, 56, 58, 62
DNA testing, 4, 14, 28, 42, 55, 56, 57, 58, 59, 60, 61, 63, 64, 65, 66, 67, 70, 71, 72, 74, 76, 77
DNA typing, 2, 4, 7, 15, 17, 28, 30, 32, 38, 49, 53, 61
DOD, 20, 21

E

exculpatory DNA, 61, 73
expungement of records, 69, 70

F

FBI, 2, 10, 11, 12, 15, 16, 17, 21, 23, 24, 27, 30, 32, 35, 42, 45, 46, 50, 54, 56
Federal Legislation, 60
felonies, 14, 16, 27, 42, 51, 53, 54, 73, 77
fingerprints, 10, 12, 13, 53, 62, 69
Forensic DNA Laboratory Improvement Program, 17, 18

G

genes, 6, 9, 38, 53
genetic testing, 33, 34, 36, 38, 39
grants, 2, 16, 18, 19, 20, 23, 24, 25, 45, 46, 49, 51, 65, 66, 67, 70, 71, 72, 76

H

homicide, 53, 70, 74
Human Genome Project, 4, 22, 31

I

identical twins, 5, 13, 31
identity, 2, 10, 14, 38, 58, 59, 63, 65, 71, 74, 77

J

juvenile delinquency, 54, 75, 76, 77

L

Law Enforcement, 23, 25, 39, 44, 67, 68, 73, 74, 76

M

markers, 6, 7, 9, 10, 12, 16, 18, 25, 29, 31, 33, 36, 47, 48, 49, 53
mitochondria, 5, 6
mitochondrial DNA, 6
mtDNA, 7, 9, 11, 14, 15, 21, 22, 29, 31
murder, 3, 16, 25, 27, 52, 53, 55, 58

N

National DNA Indexing System, 16, 45
National Institute of Justice, 10, 15, 17, 18, 19, 29, 48, 49, 54, 56, 57, 63, 68, 73
National Institute of Standards and Technology, 2, 8, 15, 20
NDIS, 16, 22, 25, 45, 48
NIJ, 2, 15, 17, 18, 19, 20, 23, 30, 49
NIST, 3, 15, 20, 30

P

paternity, 1, 3, 7, 9, 30, 36, 37
paternity cases, 3, 9
positive identification, 10, 12, 13, 33

postconviction DNA analysis, vi, 1, 3, 28, 30
postconviction testing, 41, 42, 43, 47, 56, 57, 58, 60, 61, 62, 64, 66, 68, 72, 76
prima facie, 58, 59, 63, 71, 74, 77
prosecution, 29, 58, 61, 63, 68, 72, 74, 76, 77

Q

qualifying offenses, 27, 42, 52, 53, 54, 55, 70, 74, 75, 77

R

race, 14
rape, 13, 25, 52, 62
restriction fragment length polymorphism, 8, 48
RFLP, 8, 48

S

sample collection, 7, 51, 54
sexual assault, 12, 68
short tandem repeats, 8, 48
statute of limitations, 68
STRs, 7, 8, 9, 16, 20, 25, 29, 34, 48

Supreme Court, 58
Surveillance, 28, 39, 68

T

third parties, 30, 38, 59

U

unidentified remains, 2, 14, 16, 24
United States Army, 21, 22
United States Army Criminal Investigation Laboratory, 22
universities, 23
USACIL, 3, 15, 22

V

variable number of tandem repeats, 7, 48
violence, 53, 54, 70, 75
violent crimes, 10, 14, 16, 25, 52, 53, 54
VNTRs, 7, 8, 9, 25, 29, 48

W

wrongfully convicted, 28, 30, 42, 56, 61, 64, 65, 66, 72